The Make-Believe Indian

Strider Nolan
MEDIA

Also by Jack Shakely

The Confederate War Bonnet
POWs at Chigger Lake
Che Guevara's Marijuana and Baseball Savings
and Loan
Pretty Boy Floyd's Clarinet (short stories)
The Lighthorsemen

The Make-Believe Indian

A Novel of the Indian Removal

Jack Shakely

The Make-Believe Indian. Copyright 2019 by Jack Shakely.

All Rights Reserved. No part of this book may be used or reproduced, in any manner whatsoever, without the written permission of the Author and Publisher.

Printed in the United States of America.

ISBN13: 978-1-932045-25-3
ISBN10: 1-932045-25-2
First Edition Paperback 2019

Strider Nolan Media, Inc.
6 Wyndham Way
Lancaster, PA 17601
www.stridernolanmedia.com

Dedication

To my personal Bear clan—Benton, Katie, Connor and Mason.

Acknowledgements

The factual bones of this work of fiction come from Grant Foreman's remarkable 1932 history, *Indian Removal*, which chronicles the 1830 - 1835 removal of all five civilized tribes—Cherokee, Chickasaw, Choctaw, Creek and Seminole—to Indian Territory. It is from Foreman that I first learned of the compassion of the Federal troops who accompanied the Indians on their tragic journey. Foreman is also the author of *The Five Civilized Tribes* (1934), a must-read to understand these Southern nations.

My thanks again to Zach Weingart, computer genius, who created the final manuscript.

And, as always, thank you to my muse-in-residence JoAnne Sanger, who reads every word I type and remains optimistic.

Author's Note

In 1830 President Andrew Jackson bullied through Congress the heinous and unconstitutional Indian Removal Act. The act forced all Southern Indians to abandon their traditional homes and emigrate to territories west of the Mississippi.

This cruel and deadly trek by the Cherokees became known as The Trail of Tears.

The equally devastating exodus of the Creeks, with fatalities approaching thirty percent, was called The Long Walk. This is their story.

Chapter One

Marco Secundus could remember precisely the day he decided to become an Indian.

It was the autumn of 1829. Marco was fifteen, stacking boxes of fish for the sisters of St. Matthew's Home for Boys in Cincinnati, when he glanced at the other end of the wharf and saw him. The Indian. He was tall, ramrod straight, with a scarlet turban, a small brass chest plate that caught the pale sun and sent it flying, a long white shirt, and a cornflower-blue blanket draped regally off one shoulder. He was a smear of color against the gray sky and milky-brown waters of the Ohio. He stood like an egret, a bare foot resting against the other knee, watching, waiting.

Back at the orphanage, Marco tried standing like that. It was trickier than it looked and he hopped around on one foot until he was forced to hold onto the wall beside his bed for support.

"Stop that immediately," Sister Irene said from the doorway. "You look like a crow. Now get along to the washhouse and prepare for the evening meal. You are late." She laughed. "Again."

Later that night Marco discussed his new-found ambition with a fellow orphan, Mickey Noonan. "No disrespect intended, Marco my boy," whispered Mickey. "But you're half crazy and the other half is out running around loose. You can't just decide to be an Indian. Saying you want to be an Indian makes about as much sense as me castin' aspirations to become a Chinee man. You get what you got, you know. With this red hair and what the sisters call the map of Ireland on my face, I'm a Mick, and that's a fact."

"Were you born in Ireland?" Marco asked.

"Maybe. How about you, and don't tell me a teepee."

"Beats me. I've been living here all my life. Mother Cornelia teases me and says they found me under a cabbage leaf. So I figure that if nobody knows where I came from, I get to choose, and I'm going to choose Indian."

"You look *Ital* to me. What do Indians look like?"

"I don't know a lot about Indians yet, I'll give you that," said Marco. "But I know enough to know they're from all over the place, not like Ireland, and they come in all shapes and colors. I'm going to find one that fits me and join up."

St. Matthew's Home for Boys wasn't the Ritz, but it was a long way from the Dickensian drabness of fiction. The Sisters of Carondelet, trained as nurses and teachers, ran an austere but pleasant home for some forty boys aged infant to sixteen; a school that also accepted day students; and, next door, the Carondelet Smithy and Stables that was very profitable (if pungent).

Marco was only a few months shy of sixteen and would soon outgrow, but probably never leave, St. Matt's. He had worked in the stables going on three years now, and was very good with horses. Although it was unspoken, he and the sisters both assumed that when the time came, he would take his bedroll and modest wardrobe, carry them downstairs from the orphanage to the bunkhouse behind the stables, and go to work as usual.

Marco wasn't lacking in intelligence, but he lived in the moment. After a decade of standing up straight in fresh clothes while childless couples circled him—deeming him too small, then too tall, too dark-skinned, too thin, too hungry-looking, too many teeth—he had his hopes for the future drained out of him. Rather than be angry, Marco thought they were right. He was ruthless with his self-evaluation. Who would want a nine-year-old with a cowlick? A twelve-year-old with pimples? He was always clearly unfit for adoption, wasn't he?

That's what sparked his interest in Indians. It was pretty clear to him that he didn't measure up to white man standards, but maybe Indians set the bar a little lower. They slept on the ground, he had read that, and he was pretty sure they didn't have bath tubs or even washhouses, so he thought that maybe a fellow who smelled like horses might fit right in. Hope flickered.

Marco was acknowledged as one of the best readers at St. Matt's, and he wanted to turn that skill to learning everything about Indians. But unfortunately St. Matt's entire library consisted of one shelf in the upper boys' classroom. The shelf contained three Bibles, one in Latin, a copy of *Lives of the Saints*, Blackstone's *Commentaries*, and a few well-thumbed copies of *American Magazine* that the bishop would leave on his periodic visits.

He approached Sister Irene. "Sister, I have a great desire to learn more about our Indian brethren," he said. "I have a feeling that my future may lie with these people. And I would like to ask for your help."

Sister Irene's pretty face beamed and she quietly clapped her hands. "I cannot tell you how it pleases me to hear you speak of your future, Marco. I was afraid the spark had gone out within you." She thought it over. "I know little of them myself, but I know our Lord would approve. Why go on missions to India, when Indians abound right here? Working among those noble savages is more than a job, I think, it is a calling. How may I be of assistance?"

"Take me to the library?"

The only library in Cincinnati in 1829 was what was known as a "subscription library," created by private funds and open to members only. Students and members of the clergy, however, were welcome. Sister Irene smiled. "I'd like that, Marco. You know, I've never been inside that imposing structure in all the twelve years I've been here. Not very adventurous of me, I'd say. Of course I'll take you."

The Biblio Cincinnatus was a three-story former mansion maintained by a local business guild. No match for a modern library, it was still very well stocked with encyclopedias, books—both non-fiction and fiction—as well as magazines, periodicals and newspapers from New York, Boston, even London. On the top floor were enough maps, atlases and globes to thrill any explorer. With a sprinkling of leather chairs, lamps and credenzas, it retained much of its former elegance as a men's eating club.

Although it is fairly certain that the guild fathers hadn't pictured a nun and an orphan when they included "students and clergy" in their charter, the librarian proved magnanimous, even amused, by the odd pair. Marco was awestruck by the volumes that engulfed him, but also slightly put off by the musty odor of the poorly-ventilated and sepia-toned interior. "What's that smell?" he whispered to Sister Irene as they settled into the stacks on the second floor.

"Money," Sister Irene joked, "and privilege; a

fragrance in short supply at St. Matt's."

Their weekly visits evolved into Sister Irene settling into the periodicals section on the first floor, where she pored over newspapers, especially her hometown *New York Herald*, leaving Marco free to roam the many books on the second floor. He initially rushed to novels the church might have deemed frivolous, such as James Fenimore Cooper's *Last of the Mohicans*, and William Apess' *Son of the Forest*. Written by white men who had neither the eye nor the temperament of an anthropologist, these novels nonetheless were generous in their portrayal of the Indian as intelligent, steadfast and—most of all—human.

Marco studied Colden's *History of the Iroquois Nations*, and marveled at the illustrations, but could find no one who resembled his Indian by the wharf. He enjoyed the leather-bound reports from Benjamin Hawkins to Thomas Jefferson entitled *Journal of Occurrences in the Creek Agency*. Hawkins had lived many years among the Creek and Chickasaw people and wrote in a homespun manner, replete with inventive spelling, that lent authenticity to his journals.

He finally found his turbaned hero among the many drawings and maps of *Adair's History of the American Indian* by James Adair. There was a drawing of two young men, one with a facial tattoo. Both were wearing collared shirts, and one had a kerchief knotted around his neck like a tie. And on both of their heads were turbans that would have made Ali Baba proud. The inscription read "Two men of the Choctaw nation."

Marco eventually made his way to the map room. Having only seen one Indian in his entire life, Marco was surprised at just how close many of the Indian nations were to Cincinnati: the Cherokees and Choctaws in Carolina and Georgia and the Creeks and Chickasaws in their ancestral lands starting just a hundred miles or so south of the Ohio on the Coosa and Chattahoochee rivers. Marco wondered why Indians were so scarce if they lived so near, then daydreamed that maybe they just spent most of their time being invisible to white people. He knew he would if he had the chance.

With the exception of Cooper, the books seemed rather bloodless and, in the case of Adair, fifty years old. Marco decided to bring his Indian knowledge up to date with magazines, so he joined Sister Irene in the periodicals section.

"Anything about Indians in those newspapers, Sister?" he asked idly.

"Quite a lot lately, I'm afraid."

"Afraid?"

"The stories are buried in the back of the paper, but they are there every day. Our new president Andrew

Jackson seems to have an unreasonable distaste for Indians. He even calls himself an Indian fighter. He talks with a coating of sugar, but his message is clear: whites and Indians cannot live together in peace, so the Indian must go. Jackson calls it removal, and demands that Congress deliver him a bill for Indian removal no later than next spring."

"But why remove people that are hardly there anyway? And how can you tell thousands of people to just stand up and leave? And where would they go?"

"One question at a time, please, Marco. I know this is upsetting. It seems it's not the Indian that is the problem, it's his land. The state of Georgia has already seized vast expanses of Indian land, as has Alabama."

Marco could feel his eyes starting to burn. "That isn't fair. Why don't the Indians do something? Can't they sue?"

"I'm afraid not. The scoundrels have thought of everything. Look at this." Sister Irene took a *New York Herald* down from the rack and turned to one of the back pages. "The Alabama legislators passed a law making it illegal for an Indian to sue, or even be heard as a witness, in any Alabama state court. The Indians beseech the federal government to honor its treaties, but Jackson says there is nothing he can do, these are state's rights. When I was a child in New York we used to call this find-the-pea. It was never where you thought it was."

Marco's short temper consumed him. "Now I want to be an Indian more than ever. So where does the president want to send them?"

The sister's voice was calm, attempting to keep Marco in check. "West of the Mississippi River, they say."

"But what's there?"

Sister Irene shook her head slightly. "The dark side of the moon, for all anyone knows."

Chapter Two

Sister Irene dropped her newspaper to her lap and stripped off her flimsy reading glasses. "Well, Marco, I don't know how to thank you." She laughed. "Or even whether to thank you. You and your Indians now have me preoccupied. And what I read seems ridiculously fraught. It is akin to looking up and seeing a giant rock suspended above you from a thread.

"One man says, 'That is certainly a very large rock. You should move.'

"Another man says, 'Why, I might even call it a boulder. And yet you continue to stand under it.'

"'Yes, a boulder, and just a thread,' says the first man. 'Dear me. Something should be done. Alas, I can do nothing.'

"'Nor can I,' says the other man, 'But we are in agreement that it is a boulder and quite dangerous.'

"And you say, 'But you placed the rock there. What about the thread?'

"And they say in unison, 'Yes, you should get out from under it. It's not safe for you here. Go somewhere far away.'

"Even when white men agree it is their rock, they blame the man under it. Listen to what Congress did last week: it agreed that because all lands west of the Mississippi are the property of the federal government, it would therefore guarantee every Indian man emigrating there a new rifle, blankets, provisions for his family for a year and a military escort from the western banks of the Mississippi, through Little Rock in the Arkansas sector, to their final destination in what Congress is now calling Indian Territory. Then they patted themselves on the back and called it a day."

Marco looked puzzled. "But what about east of the Mississippi, the first part of the journey? If the Indians decide to go, how do they get to the Mississippi? That's got to be a thousand miles away, isn't it?"

"I'm not sure they get to decide to go," Sister Irene said. "I believe Andrew Jackson will have something to say about that. He says the Indian *must* go, although Congress says not so fast." She rummaged through the pages of the *Herald*. "Here it is. These very words: 'Provided, however, that this Act shall not be construed so as to compel any Indian to emigrate, but they shall be free to go or stay, as they please.' The poor Indian asks 'What about the boulder hanging from the thread? Do I plant for next year? And where? Who will feed my children?' The waiting and wondering must be awful.

"It is like being a child in bed and hearing your parents fight," she continued. "Regardless of the winner, it frightens you and you fear you will be the loser. Jackson gets his Indian Removal Act passed, then Congress dilutes it, then the Supreme Court rules that the act is unconstitutional and the Indians may remain. Jackson is furious and says that's the Supreme Court's decision, but let's see it enforce it. 'Here's what I'm going to do', Jackson says. 'I'm giving the Indians five years to hie themselves across the Mississippi voluntarily, or I will escort them there myself, at the point of a spear if necessary.'"

"Five years is a long time," Marco said.

"Maybe when you are fifteen," Sister Irene replied.

Chapter Three

The largest horse auction of the 1831 season was held in Port William, twenty miles south of Cincinnati on the Kentucky side of the Ohio River.

White Kentucky and Tennessee horsemen brought out their two-year-old thoroughbreds for their first viewing. Indians brought their ponies to sell and swap. Port William doubled in size overnight, the racetrack was busy from dawn to dusk, the stands were full, and intense betting was the order of the day. Food stalls and patent medicine shows dotted the margins, insuring plenty to eat and drink. (Pinkham's Herbal Tonic, for example, was about half alcohol. Booze was the "secret elixir" in all patent medicines of the time). There was a fair-like atmosphere of the 1831 auction enjoyed by both Indians and whites that gave no clue that it would be the last of its kind.

Brother Bartholomew set up his shoeing stall near the race track as always. Instead of relying on the Port William blacksmith, who always hiked his prices come auction time, the brother brought everything he'd need with him. Marco gained enormous respect for the sinewy little man as the youth half-carried, half-dragged an enormous carpetbag, struggling to keep up with the blacksmith who carried his own carpetbag as if he were out for a stroll. Marco learned that a carpetbag full of horseshoes was as heavy as a carpetbag full of anvils, if there was such a thing, but his enthusiasm was unflagging. He was so excited, he felt he could have carried horseshoes with the horses still attached all the way to Mobile.

After getting everything in place, Marco failed completely at trying to look calm, and burst into a half giggle, half shout. "Mind if I take a little look around, Brother Bart? Just to get my bearings?"

Brother Bartholomew smiled broadly as he leaned a hand-painted sign of a horseshoe against one of the now-empty carpetbags on the table. "Sure, Marco. You can do me a big favor at the same time. When-ever you see a few men congregating, please inform them that Brother Bart's Horseshoe Emporium is now open for business at the first turn, as usual. And if you are still in search of some Indian folks, you might try the stand of oaks behind the holding pens. Here's a dime in case you want to try some of the Indian bread they sell over there. Good luck."

Young Marco tried rather unsuccessfully not to run or skip, so overcome was he with curiosity. He patted his pocket from time to time to make sure his ten-cent piece was secure. He had no interest in spending it for food—he could eat another day—but money in his pocket was something altogether new. He felt empowered.

He also felt at home with the horses, and many of these mounts were far superior to the carriage horses he saw at the Carondelet stables. He nuzzled a big roan in the paddock.

"Can't say you know much about horses,"said one of the dirtiest boys Marco had ever seen, "but if you want to throw away your money, I'll give you two to one. He goes off in the next race."

"Get downwind, you scamp," Marco said idly. "Your smell might get the horses riled."

"Who are you, Sir Bathes-a-lot? I smell like any other back stretch boy," the newcomer said, jutting his jaw in defiance. "You try muckin' out stables all day, and see how you like it. You want to place a bet or not, dumbbell?"

"Dumbbell, is it? Horses talk to me," Marco said. "Smells like you been talking to the wrong end. I'm not usually a betting man, but I'd bet ten cents on this one, just to shut you up."

"A whole dime? Well, times is tough. Show me your money."

Marco casually took the coin from his pocket, immediately ruing that he had been goaded into risking his newfound fortune.

They turned to the rail. Soon they watched the pennant-festooned starting rope lift with the crack of a pistol, and the horses bolted away. To Marco's pleasure, his horse won by four lengths going away.

"Well, shite, even a blind pig can find an acorn once in a while," said the smelly boy. "Lucky for me we didn't shake on it. See ya later, sucker."

"Pay the young man his money, Skeeter," came a thunderous voice behind Marco. "The odds were four to one, I believe."

Marco turned and there he was, his Indian, tall and straight as a Georgia pine. He was wearing a white turban this time with a palmetto buckle, but the rest was just like those two men in the etching in the Adair book.

"Aw, Mister Coachman, we was only funnin'. I ain't got but a dime, sir, I swear." The boy named Skeeter held it out as proof.

The Indian scooped the dime up and handed it to the dumbfounded Marco. "Get out of here, Skeeter, you little thief. Here you are, fellow. I'd say you were lucky, except for the way I saw you with Amber King before the race. You know your horses. I think Amber King ran that race for you as much as for me. I just so happen to be his owner."

Wide-eyed, Marco blurted, "Pardon me, sir. Are you a man of the Choctaw nation?"

The man laughed heartily. "No reason to be afraid.

But I'm Creek. John Coachman by name. And you are?"

"Marco Secundus, sir, under the employ of Brother Bartholomew of the Carondelet stables."

"Well, if that don't beat the band. He's the very fellow I'm looking for. Got a couple of ponies that need shoeing. They aren't in Amber King's class, mind you, but they'll do in front of some fancy lady's shay." He paused, studying Marco. "Why do you keep staring at me? Never met a rich Indian before?"

Marco's face flushed. "Never met a poor one, either. I'm sorry, sir. I'm just real curious because I come from the orphanage and I think there may be some Indian in me, too."

"Glad to hear you say that, son. Being Indian ain't too popular nowadays. I wish there was some Indian in everybody, including yon Andrew Jackson. Then he'd have to kill himself or send himself out west." He smiled. "Either way, we'd be ahead. Lead on, my fellow Indian, and show me to Brother Bartholomew."

Brother Bart was busy shoeing a big bay under the watchful eye of its corpulent owner.

"Halloo, Brother Bartholomew," John Coachman shouted. "Good news. I paid the ransom on your assistant and here he is." He turned to the fat man. "Good day, Mister Oliver."

Brother Bart, with two horseshoe nails clinched

between his teeth, nodded pleasantly.

The corpulent man was not at a loss for words, however. "Hello, there, Coachman, or Co-cha-ma, or whatever you are calling yourself these days. I hear your big red horse just won a race."

"Who's Co-cha-ma?" asked a confused Marco.

"I'll explain later," Coachman said under his breath, then turned back. "Why, yes, sir, Mister Oliver. Maybe this is my lucky day."

"It might be at that. I'm always on the lookout for good horse flesh. Is he for sale? 'Course it might seem a shame, separating a red man from his red horse. Like breaking up a set." Oliver laughed uproariously at his feeble joke.

"Always a bundle of mirth, Mister Oliver," said John Coachman. "Well, to answer your question, we are at a horse auction, where horses are traded and sold, and although I haven't put Amber King up for bid, I would seriously consider any offer over one hundred dollars."

The fat man whistled. "Too rich for my blood." He paused. "Maybe I'll just wait three or four years and you'll be selling him ten cents on the dollar as you pack up for a trip across the Mississippi."

Coachman's voice took on a steel edge. "I see your understanding of politics is as dismal as your stable of losers, Thaddeus. My farm is twice the size of yours. I'm going nowhere. Brother Bartholomew, I shall return when you stick those nails where they belong."

Marco walked beside the tall man, his thirst for things Indian far from satisfied. "Why did he call you Co-cha-ma, Mister Coachman? Respectfully, sir, you told me you would tell me later. Is this a good time?"

"Co-cha-ma is my Creek name, Marco. I use it with my mother and her clan." He laughed softly. "And sometimes in horse trading when I want the white man to think he is dealing with a dumb savage." He waved Marco on. "Come along. Want some fry bread? My treat."

They walked to the grove of trees mentioned by Brother Bart. A dozen or so Indians, most in conventional white man's attire of collared shirts and long pants, readied their ponies for the auction. Marco was a bit disappointed that the dress wasn't more festive, but he made no comment.

They settled on a bench under a shade tree. Marco liked the taste of fry bread, sort of a cross between a pretzel and corn bread. If this is what Indians eat, I'll be just fine, Marco thought.

"Mister Coachman, why was that fat Mister Oliver mean to you? Why did he say he'd buy your horse for ten cents on the dollar?"

"It's all about distant drums, my new friend, and they are sending confusing messages." Coachman sighed. "It's this damned Indian Removal Act. Congress says it would love to see us leave, but it is voluntary, and if we go, there will be free land and game and fish in great abundance waiting for us on the other side of the river. President Jackson says removal is mandatory and we have five years to clear out. And get this: the Supreme Court just ruled that the whole idea of removal is not just stupid, it's unconstitutional. But Jackson says he's going to do it anyway."

Coachman picked up a stick and started making curlicues in the dirt at his feet. "It reminds me of a story my grandmother told us when we were children. A mighty chief had vanquished another tribe and he came to put their head man to death. The defeated brave stood before the chief and said, 'Killing me would be a mistake, Mighty One. I possess a special gift'

"'What sort of gift?' asked the curious chief.

"'I have a special gift with horses. Leave me one of your good horses, and in two years I will teach it to talk, just like you and me.'

"'Kill you now or kill you later, makes no difference to me. Give this fool a horse,' the chief said and trotted away.

"'Oh husband,' said the woman by the brave's side, 'I rejoice that you remain alive, but that was a very stupid thing to say.'

"'Maybe not so stupid,' said the man. 'In two years the chief might die; in two years I might die; or this damn horse might talk.'

"So I figure in five years Andrew Jackson might die; in five years Jackson might not be reelected; or the Supreme Court might raise an army."

Chapter Four

Farms in horse country have never really been farms, not even in the early nineteenth century. They are well-groomed meadows with stables and a workout track on one end. Add a fruit orchard nearby and you had Sunrise Farm twenty miles south of Tullahoma, Tennessee, near the Alabama border.

Sunrise Farm was established by John Coachman's father, Caleb, in 1788 in what was known as Creek Country or Southwest Territory, years before the state of Tennessee was established. Caleb fell in love and married Haya-Atke, a Creek woman whose name means "first light of dawn." They produced two children: John and Susana. Susana died in infancy. Caleb passed when John was just twenty.

John Coachman was what was called in those days a *meti*, what would be called mixed-blood today. His ability, as he put it, "to talk like a white man and think like a Creek," served him well and he prospered. He built a large clapboard house which, to his surprise, displeased his mother. "This is a building for white *miccos*, white kings, not for children of the earth like me. I am uncomfortable," she told him in Creek. So John built a cluster of cabins near the orchard and original homestead in the Creek manner for his mother, her sister and a floating number of uncles, cousins and other members of the Wind clan.

Returning from the Port William horse auction, Coachman noticed that Co-cha-ma Town (as his mother had dubbed it) was more full of children than usual. But he was busy running stables and keeping his dozen or so employees (most of whom were the same clan members living in the little village) fed and clothed. Then, three months later, returning from another horse auction in Lexington, he noticed that three new double cabins were nestled a few hundred yards away in the woods. On close inspection, he found a half-dozen pine poles, one already stripped of bark, in a brambles by the stream. He called a clan meeting.

"My dear mother, my honored aunts, uncles and cousins, you know you are welcome here as long as there is breath in me. If we need to grow bigger, we will grow bigger. Do not fear. I will help you build. We are Wind clan together." There was a murmur of approving grunts, which was about as much praise as Coachman was going to get, and he knew it.

"But please, may I ask," Coachman continued, "why are we now so many? Why are there so many more children? Some of you look hungry; some of you look sick. Is there an illness among our people? Speak to me plainly."

"They chase us, Co-cha-ma," came a man's voice in the rear.

"Who chases you?"

"The Alabama white men," said the stable foreman, Uncle Hes-se, in the Creek language. "Two years ago, you know, we signed a treaty giving the Alabama chiefs much land in exchange for their promise to leave us in peace. But this did not fill their bellies, it made them thirst like mad dogs for more. They swoop down on us like a rainstorm. They come to our poor towns with papers and whiskey." He grunted loudly. "They say sign the paper, we give you whiskey. And my eyes fill with tears when I say they almost never leave disappointed. Then they come back and say now we must leave, the paper says so. I have seen this."

John Coachman felt his throat tighten. "I was one of the signers of that treaty. It promised peace. Can't the Alabama militia protect our people?"

His mother, Haya-Atke said, "They *are* the militia, John. Something has changed. These are not your father's white men. I admired them so, my son. Your father and his fellows were creating a new nation of big ideas, full of light and good will. No longer. Today they are filled with dark greed and anger. And they have permission from their chiefs. Jackson hates the

Indian, that is known. They say a fish rots from the head. I believe it is so."

John Coachman said, "My brothers and sisters, we will build a safe town. Right here. There is abundant water and game and I own the land for as far as the eye can see. We will plant corn and sorghum." He laughed. "Soon we will all be eating as well as my horses." There was a ripple of appreciative yips. "The white man will not bother us here. I can read his papers and push them in his face. I have done it before. Let us grow a big town. Our grandfathers and children will be safe here." He held his arms open. "Let's begin today. A new town deserves a new name. What shall it be?"

His mother's sister, Rabbit, said softly, "Hope Town. It may be the only place we find it."

Marco, with just a little help from Sister Irene, wrote John Coachman a letter reiterating his newfound belief that he was also part Indian, and said that he was more than willing to apprentice himself to Coachman's stables. He enumerated the skills he had learned under Brother Bartholomew and said he would be willing to begin his apprenticeship immediately. After a glacial two weeks, Marco received a large manila packet from John Coachman of Sunrise Farm, Tennessee. Coachman said he remembered

Marco well, that there was no finer teacher than Brother Bartholomew, and that a young horseman apprentice might indeed be welcome. But, Coachman went on, Marco had admitted that the sum of his knowledge about Indians came from books, and that a two-year apprenticeship among strangers with strange voices, strange food and strange habits might be too much to bear. "In addition," Coachman wrote, "don't forget the distant drums I spoke of when first we met. It is winter now and there is little to do. If you haven't changed your mind, come spend a couple of months with me in March. You can help me with the yearlings and mares. Perhaps you can even renew your friendship with Amber King. If you decide to return to Cincinnati, I will think no less of you. I have enclosed a few things to help in your decision-making. I await your answer."

Inside the packet were maps, a recent inventory of the Sunrise horse stock, and ten silver dollars in a small leather pouch. Marco took the packet to his room at the far end of the stable, sat on his bed and silently wept. He was an orphan no longer. Someone wanted him.

Chapter Five

When Marco arrived at Sunrise Farm he found himself pleasantly lodged between two worlds.

John Coachman took Marco's shoulders in greeting. "Marco, we'll make a few changes while you are here. You will stay with me in the big house, not in the stables or the village. All the stable men, including boss Uncle Hes-se, speak mainly Creek. Indians like to have fun, and they will tease you at first. I will warn Uncle Hes-se to go light on you, but unfortunately he is a prankster himself. Give them a few days, they will see your way with horses and respect you. Also I couldn't ask you to sleep in the village for the same reason. You are only a book Indian. It would be like asking you to sleep in France."

Coachman got very serious. "But I want you to spend as much time as you can in the village. My mother speaks perfect English and she has offered to be your teacher about the ways of the Muscogee. That is what we call ourselves in our language. Much to learn." He laughed. "And lastly, I want you in the big house so I can have someone to talk with at dinner."

It didn't take long for Marco to earn the respect of Uncle Hes-se and the stable boys. One morning as Marco was brushing a young stallion, two of the Indian grooms dropped a large but harmless garden snake into the stall to frighten the city boy. As luck would have it, Marco was turned the other way and didn't see the snake.

But the skittish horse did, and reared in panic, spinning and driving Marco painfully into the side of the stall. Never flinching, Marco dropped the brush and grabbed the wild-eyed stallion by the neck. Marco put his mouth next to the flailing horse's ear, its feet often flying out from under, and calmly talked the big animal through its panic. Finally, his right hand still guiding the horse by the ear, Marco led the horse away from the stall and into the paddock. There, fighting nausea from pain in his torso, he patted and walked the two-year old horse.

Uncle Hes-se approached with a halter and relieved the young man of his charge. He put his hand on Marco's shoulder. "You good with horse," he said. "You horse talker. You Indian for sure." Then he turned and, with a withering tirade in Creek, drew the two shamefaced men to stand in front of Marco and mumble something Marco assumed was an apology. Marco waved his arm nonchalantly in acknowledgement, and nearly fainted from pain. He had sprained two ribs.

Marco did visit the village, first shyly with John Coachman leading the way, then alone and whenever he could. Marco was fascinated with Haya-Atke. The only women he had ever known were the sisters of St. Matt's, primarily Sister Irene. This feisty, intelligent woman who seemed perfectly at ease in whatever language or world she chose captivated him. Haya-Atke sensed Marco's admiration and was quick to respond in kind.

One night at dinner in the big house she said, "Marco, I agree that you are Indian, a little bit *meti*, just enough. You are Wind clan now, if you wish. I say you are my family. I will be your grandmother. I will teach you, I will care for you, I will give you our old ways food and medicine to make you strong. And I have been listening to what they say about you at the stables. You have earned the respect of Uncle Hes-se. We have talked and agreed that I should give you your secret warrior name to protect you. From this night forward, you will be *Iyabi-Corakko*, Horse Talker. You will continue to be Marco, of course, but deep inside your heart you will be Iyabi-Corakko. I will tell the horses. They will like your new name."

Marco sputtered. "Yes, I wish that. I wish with all my heart. I ... I...."

Seeing that Marco was on the verge of embarrassing tears, John Coachman stepped in and decided to lighten the mood. "That is quite an honor, Horse Talker. I am sorry that a raise in salary does not accompany the honor, but times are tough." He laughed casually. "So. Marco Secundus. Does that name have special meaning?"

"Far from it," Marco answered, recovering a little. "When the sisters at St. Mathew's found me one morning on their front steps, there was a note pinned to my blanket. 'His name is Marco,' is all the note said."

"And where did Secundus come from?"

Marco flashed a wry smile. "Mother Cornelia said I was the second baby left at the orphanage that day."

"I will never understand orphanages," Haya-Atke said.

"No? I see many children in the village," Marco noted. "And I have read in the newspapers that many Indians are being sent away, whole villages being burned to the ground, families starving, others running away. I guess I just thought that some of these village children are orphans. Are there no Indian orphanages?"

"No, my son," Haya-Atke answered quietly.

John Coachman looked deeply into the young man's eyes, not wanting to cause pain with raw truth. "I think orphanages are the white man's burden, Marco, born in cities out of loneliness and despair. We live in farms and villages where you know every member of your clan and your clan will watch over you." He chuckled. "Sometimes whether you like it or not. But imagine a poor woman in New York, or Cincinnati, sick, alone, hungry, with no way to care for her baby. She does a brave and tragic thing in order to save her child: she gives it up. It is a decision Indians like my mother may misread, but I think it is honorable. You live, my friend, because someone sacrificed her own happiness for yours."

Still filled with emotion, Marco didn't dare lift his eyes. Instead he talked to his spoon. "When you are an orphan, all you think about is being an orphan, and how you should be better, or smarter, or tougher. If I ever thought of my parents, which was almost never, I thought of them throwing me away. And I didn't blame them. I figured I must be lacking something, and when adults came to the orphanage and circled me like a horse in the paddock only to leave me alone, I thought I must work harder than boys outside. That's why I learned to read and write and do my numbers before I was ten. I learned to be the best horseman Brother Bartholomew ever met. I read the entire Bible by the time I was twelve. I read Shakespeare." He lifted his eyes and smiled. "Have any questions about *Hamlet*?"

"Tell me the story in Creek," Coachman teased.

"Give me a month."

*   *   *

Near the end of Marco's probationary month as an Indian, John Coachman was visited by the principal chief of the Creek Lower Towns, Eneah Micco. Micco had been a staunch advocate for his people to remain in their ancestral homes, but now he was wavering.

Sitting at the trestle table in the big house dining room, the old chief pulled his shawl around his shoulders and stared out the window at the blustery meadow. The morning was still teetering between winter and spring.

"I don't understand, Co-cha-ma. Everything I do with the white man seems to be wrong. It's like quicksand; the more I struggle, the deeper I sink."

"How so, chief?" said Coachman.

"Last winter I presented Secretary of War Eaton a list of 1,400 white intruders who had violated our treaties and settled in the Lower Towns. I gave names and homesteads. Eaton wrote that these violations were further proof of how helpless both the Creek and federal governments are to stop such evils, and could be remedied only by our leaving. He wrote that the American people do not understand why their most generous offer of free abundant land where there is no white man is being refused. John Ridge helped me write a fine letter back saying how can we accept something that we have never seen? Would you give away your house, the house of your grandfathers, for a house far away in an unknown land? And you are not giving us land, you are trading us a land of mystery for the land of our birth. It was a good letter, but it, too, bit me."

The chief retrieved a letter from under his shawl. "Here is the letter Secretary Eaton wrote in return. I wanted your thoughts on it. He wrote a similar letter to Chief Opathle Yahola of the Upper Creeks, Chief LeFlore of the Choctaws, and George Gains of the Cherokees. He says the Great Father would never send us blindly into our new lands, and he would provide one thousand dollars to outfit an exploratory party to visit our new land, to see for ourselves its many riches and to select choice spots for our new villages. He says that the expedition will be led by Colonel John Coffee of the American Army, with soldiers from the engineers corps to make maps and insure our safety. He says that our refusal to undertake such an expedition will be further evidence that we care little for our people or their future."

He folded the letter back into his tunic. "John, we must go, of course. But I am too old to go on such a trip. Will you go in my stead?"

"Of course I will, Chief. It is an honor. But I have a few questions. Will our agreement to join the expedition seal our fate? I do not believe that the federal government has the power or the gumption to displace thousands of law-abiding men, women and children. But is this expedition part of Jackson's plan to entice us away? Is this the carrot before the stick?" Before the chief could respond, Coachman added, "And on a less important level, such a trip will take long preparation. And I have a farm to run. Does Secretary Eaton have a departure date in mind?"

"That is all to be worked out when we agree. As to your other questions, I will tell you, I am just a farmer who was elected chief. I am a man of the earth, not the statehouse. Opathle Yahola is such a man and he says that in time we must go; it is written in stone." He paused and looked around the dining room to make sure they were alone. "I am uncertain. But for the expedition itself, I am less interested in *when* than in *who*. I don't trust those white soldiers to report honestly. They are making the trip already dedicated to seeing us leave. Their eyes will be dimmed by certainty. John, you once said that you could speak like a white man and think like a Creek. That is just what we need. Are there any more of you, someone who could accompany you and write observations and reports, someone we can trust?"

Coachman drummed his fingers on the table. "I am thinking of one. I'm not sure he will say yes, but if he does, he is a white man, he reads and writes, he almost thinks like an Indian, and he talks to horses."

Chapter Six

As the days grew longer, Marco spent most evenings after work in the village. The men mostly ignored him, but Haya-Atke and the women were willing tutors. They were amused, and a little flattered, to see a white man learning to be an Indian.

Marco learned the names of animals like *efu* (dog), *cufe/coofay* (rabbit), and *nokose* (bear). He learned every part of a horse from its *yopo* (nose) to its *ena* (tail). This almost impressed Uncle Hes-se, who passed by the old house's front porch during a language lesson and said "Heres-chi" out of the corner of his mouth.

"Uncle Hes-se says very good, Marco," said Haya-Atke. "High praise."

Being a spoken language at the time, Creek was more rudimentary than English in some ways, but just as beautiful. Marco learned that the same word could have different meanings depending on the words it was paired with or the situation. The word *Eneah*, for instance, the first name of the principal chief at the time, could mean fat, or lard, or grease depending on whether you were talking about a man, a frying pan, or a wagon wheel.

John Coachman poked his head into Haya-Atke's kitchen one afternoon where Marco was learning about, and tasting, some Creek foods like *sofki*, the hominy-based porridge that was a staple of the Creek diet. "Don't forget to teach him stuff he can really use, Mother, like *hom-pac-chi*."

Marco looked up curiously. "What does that mean, Grandmother?"

"Let's eat," she said with a twinkle.

John Coachman walked onto the workout track to find Marco atop Amber King, the big stallion, the two deep in conversation. With the morning fog still covering the horse's withers, Marco bent over Amber King's neck, whispering encouragement as they started around the track. They trotted ghost-like around the first turn, then started into a canter just as the sun broke through. When they hit the final turn, the morning sun shone bright and Amber King was flying. John Coachman checked his stopwatch and smiled.

"That last quarter mile would have won the Lexington Heats last year," Coachman said as he approached horse and rider as Marco dismounted. Amber King playfully nudged Marco on the shoulder, causing him almost to stumble into his boss. "I've known other men who are good with horses, but Amber King knows you do more than just talk to him; you listen. Now that you are here and working so well together, I dearly wish we could run him in one of the big races this year. But I am forbidden from entering a horse because of this Indian blood nonsense."

They walked the big red horse back to the stable. "Marco, Amber King's racing days may be over for a while, but he and I have important work to do, and I think you might just fit in. I know you've only been here a few months, but you are my best horseman. And don't worry about your struggles with our language; I need a man who speaks English."

Together they brushed down Amber King, who stood as if he were posing for his own statue. "How can I fit in, sir?" Marco asked.

"Well, I've been asked to head a delegation of various Indian tribes to visit territories west of the Mississippi that the federal government has set aside for Indian occupation. There will be Cherokees, Chickasaws, Choctaws, and Creeks, a virtual Indian Tower of Babel. I want you along to care for Amber King, of course, but I also want you to get to know the soldiers and engineers who will come with us. You are white, and just for a while I want you to act white; act like you are one of them observing us, not one of us watching them. Observe, listen and record. Draw maps. Note what official reports will not show. Little things."

Coachman continued, "This will be an important mission, but I can't promise it will be an easy one. This is above and beyond an apprenticeship, so you will get paid just like the other horsemen. But the pay is not very good, the food is likely to be worse, the conditions will be rough, and we will be there well into the winter. As I said, this is outside of our understanding of your apprenticeship. If you would rather not join me, I will understand completely. You can continue to stay at Sunrise Farm and practice being a Creek, or I will pay for your return to Cincinnati and Brother Bart, and you can come back next year. Please consider my offer, Marco. That is all I ask."

"Thank you, Mr. Coachman, I will consider it." He paused, then smiled. "Okay, you can count me in."

Chapter Seven

In 1825, the Creek Nation was betrayed from within.

Sensing the increasing pressure from the white man to accept individual allotments, the nation's chiefs met in council the year before to set forth a declaration for the future.

They made their destiny clear. "On a deep and solemn reflection, we have, with one voice, decided to follow the pattern of the Cherokees, and on no account whatever will we consent to sell one square foot of our land, neither by exchange nor otherwise. We want the talk to be straight, that the land will remain as it is, in common, and as it always has been." The declaration went on to say that if any chief should "break these laws," he would be executed.

It would take a fool, or someone taking a bribe so large it was worth risking death, to violate that declaration. William McIntosh was both.

McIntosh was a mixed-blood town chief who owned a tavern in Georgia. He was ambitious and greedy, and thought he could parlay white ignorance of Indian ways into a fortune for himself. Knowing the United States government's preference for treating with the head man, whether a king or president, McIntosh decided to give the white man just that. With no authority whatsoever, he presented himself to Indian Commissioner John Crowell as chief of the Creek nation (there was no such position), ready to enter into an agreement ceding lands to Georgia. With money secretly provided him by Georgia officials, McIntosh bribed a dozen lower chiefs and fifty hangers-on to pretend they represented the entire nation; and in February, 1828, they signed the Treaty of Indian Springs, trading more than a million acres of prime Georgia land in exchange for land they had never seen.

The treaty was ratified in Washington, but it took months for most Creeks to learn of the treachery. Opathle Yahola warned McIntosh that death awaited him if he "signed that paper," without knowing it was already signed and approved by Congress.

McIntosh feared for his life, of course, but Commissioner Crowell gave McIntosh $25,000 (about $300,000 at current rates) and the sworn United States government's guarantee that McIntosh would be protected.

That guarantee, like so many others, was hollow. In August, Chief Menawa and about 100 Okfuskees surrounded the McIntosh home at dawn. After telling the women and children to leave the building, Menawa and his men burned down the house and shot dead McIntosh and another signer of the treaty, Etommee Tustennuggee. The next day Sam Hawkins, McIntosh's son-in-law and a signatory of the treaty, was captured and hanged in the square of Wetumpka Town. Sam's brother Ben was shot a few days later, but survived and escaped to Texas.

Chilly McIntosh, William's son, and a large group that became known as the McIntosh Creeks figured that they had better emigrate or be killed. Undoubtedly using leftover bribe money, Chilly hired the steamship Fidelity to transport about seven hundred ill-prepared clan members up the Mississippi and the Arkansas to the Grand River, near the recently-established Fort Gibson, in what would become Indian Territory.

The winter of 1829 was bitterly cold, and nature exhibited its cruel Rule of Three. About a third, mainly relatively prosperous mixed-bloods, went north along the Verdigris River to eke out a living that in only a few years would return them to their former prosperity. Another third, mostly children and the elderly, died from starvation, freezing weather or whooping cough. The final third, mostly full-bloods, simply gave up. They clustered around Fort Gibson begging for food, begging for whiskey; as a writer from *Nile's Weekly* reported, "wandering about like bees whose hive has been destroyed."

It was this dejected collection of beggars, whores, drunks and lost souls who greeted John Coachman and Marco Secundus in 1832.

When John and Marco arrived in Memphis, the Army's Colonel Coffee and his men were already on board the steamship Galahad. George Gaines, representing the Cherokees, was also there, and furious. He met Coachman at the dock, followed by an obviously chagrined Coffee.

"John, old friend. First, here is the good news: the federal government has graciously provided all our ponies ample supplies of hay and grain to last them through the winter. Here is the bad news: they didn't allocate a penny for food for you and me. Not a loaf of bread, not a pound of bacon. Nothing."

Coachman turned his eyes to the Army officer. "Is this true?"

"I'm afraid it is," replied the red-faced colonel. "The hay and oats, as well as the horses and mules themselves, I personally secured from the cavalry stores right here in Memphis. But to buy foodstuffs for our journey, which I thought would be simple, takes a great deal of money, perhaps two hundred dollars; and as I understand it, the money promised you, the thousand dollars, is attached to another Indian bill in Congress and is stuck in committee."

"How long will it take to get it unstuck?" Coachman asked.

George Gaines, who had served one term as a congressman from Kentucky, grumbled. "Who knows. I'm not blaming poor Colonel Coffee." He turned and faced the officer. "It's not your fault. It's this damn do-nothing Congress. Congress is going on summer recess this week, and when it returns in September, it will have a stack of pork barrel bills as tall as a man. And some of my old Washington friends tell me that any bill providing relief to the Indian, regardless of how small, is meeting strong opposition from the Georgia, Alabama and Mississippi delegations. They claim that any help to the Indian just coddles us and allows us to go on suckling the government teat. You and I could wind up spending Christmas in Memphis. Of course, by that time, the Galahad—and I suspect, Colonel Coffee and his men—will be long gone."

"This is serious," said Coachman. "When McCurtain and his Chickasaws arrive here and find no food, they will fly into anger, and probably turn for home on the spot. And the stories they will bring back with them will freeze his people: 'The government wants to starve us, there is no food in that hole they call our new home,' and so forth. McCurtain didn't want to come anyway, but was afraid the Cherokees would get the pick of the litter." He became quiet in thought. "Colonel Coffee, would you be willing to sacrifice two horses to insure the success of our expedition?"

Coffee cocked his head in uncertainty. "Army horses are easy to come by while we are still here in Memphis, but Mr. Coachman, my soldiers won't eat a horse, and I won't make them."

"I'm not talking about eating them, I'm talking about trading them. I'll even throw a pony of my own into the pot. My wrangler Marco is a horse talker. Why, he'll sweet talk those horses into becoming flour and rice, beef and bacon, and enough beans to feed a brigade. We will welcome McCurtain with a shipload of grub."

The food in the dining room of the Galahad was plentiful, well-prepared and free to the delegates. Colonel Coffee contracted with the steamship owners for full payment and a ten percent bonus upon the boat's safe return.

Dinner the first night was an ode to opulence. There was lobster in cream, oysters on the half shell, tomato aspic, quail, asparagus, and bottles of wine.

Marco had actually eaten oysters and asparagus, but the rest he hated on sight. The quail looked like a fat sparrow to him. Who the hell would eat that?

Nor was he interested in the wine. When he was twelve he and Mickey had stolen a bottle of sacramental wine and drank the entire thing behind the stable. Marco didn't throw up but Mickey did, and it was a smell he would forever associate with the beverage.

Marco decided this would be a good time to meet some of the enlisted men as John Coachman had suggested. He grabbed a loaf of bread and a large sausage and headed down to the barn-like first level of the boat. Like horsemen everywhere, the soldiers were grooming and blanketing their ponies, preparing them for their first night on the river. The horses could not see the water and were docile, lulled by the constant rhythmic slapping of the paddles as the boat headed to Little Rock.

"Hello, fellows," Marco said brightly. "That dining room is too rich for my blood, so I thought I'd check on my ponies and eat down here." He held up the bread and sausage like fresh kill. "There's plenty for you, too, if you've a mind to."

The three young men just stood there, stupefied. Finally, one of the soldiers pointed his brush at Marco. "Well, hell and damnation. You speak American. I didn't think Indians did that. You Indian?"

"I'm as Indian as I'll ever be," Marco said with a cheerful smile. "You hungry?"

Chapter Eight

While the expedition members rested and readied themselves at Fort Smith for their venture into the unknown, Colonel Coffee ordered two soldiers ahead to alert the garrison commander at Fort Gibson. Colonel Coffee wanted no surprises. Fort Gibson had been created, after all, to serve the various Indian nations Congress convinced itself would momentarily be arriving in their new territory.

On a prearranged signal from John Coachman, Marco approached the Colonel. "Mind if I tag along, sir? I speak English as well as Creek. Maybe I could be of some help if there are Indians near the fort."

"My field reports tell me there are," Coffee said, "and they seem to be in dire condition. No one understands their language. They are free to leave, but they cluster about the fort like a litter of pups that has lost its mother. Yes, go to them with my thanks. Talk to them and listen well. How can we hope to help ten thousand if a mere hundred befuddle us?"

Marco, along with the "hell and damnation"

sergeant whose name turned out to be Blackstock, and a soldier no older than Marco named Ochs, ferried across the Arkansas to the mouth of the Grand River where Fort Gibson stood on the bluff.

The stench of humanity hit them even before they saw the fort. And what they saw unnerved them. "Jesus, Mary and Joseph," the sergeant said, then silently covered his mouth and nose with his kerchief, and kicked his horse into a trot. Ochs was a little more demonstrative. He rode alongside his superior.

"Sergeant, permission to ride like demons to the fort, deliver our message, and get the hell out of here. This smells like death, Sergeant. Sickness, vomit and death."

"Keep your poise, soldier," Blackstock said. "We will enter the fort with the dignity of soldiers. I've seen this before—maybe not quite this bad—among camp followers everywhere. It's the whiskey, of course. It grabs these poor devils by the throat. They will die cold and naked with an empty bottle of whiskey in their hand. Mister Secundus, will you join us?"

"Thank you, Sergeant, but Colonel Coffee and my boss John Coachman want me to spend time with these people. Gather information and listen to how we may be of assistance. I will meet you here at the ferry for the afternoon run back to Fort Smith."

*   *   *

It was dark when Marco returned to Fort Smith. He found John Coachman, Menawa, and the other member of the Creek delegation, Creek lawman Buck Tom (he of the lighthorsemen who, among his other skills, was said to be able to start a campfire in a tornado). The three men were smoking pipes and drinking coffee.

"Well, Marco," Coachman said. "Did you find Indians there? Are they as poor as Colonel Coffee says?"

"They are well beyond poor, sir. What I found was disturbing. Maybe it's because I was brought up by the sisters, but I have to ask: When does a man stop being a man? There should be a spark within us. But not these people. Whiskey has stolen the spark from these wretches. They are not just beyond poor, they are beyond hope."

"Are they Creek?" asked Buck Tom.

"Yes. My Creek is still limited, but I understood most of the words. I asked if they were Creek, and a young man said yes. He had no teeth, Mister Coachman, no teeth at all. I asked him what clan they were and he said *Mak-en-tosh*. I think that is what he said."

"The McIntoshes," Coachman said softly.

"They will kill me," old Chief Menawa said equally softly. "I am dead to them."

"I'm sorry, Micco, but you did not see them," Marco said. "I did. If any one of them had a pistol, he would hand it to you and ask you to shoot him. They don't have the courage to die, much less kill."

"You don't understand Indian ways," Menawa said. "Revenge runs deep. It only takes one. I killed William McIntosh and two members of his family. They richly deserved to die, but drunk or sober, someone will try to avenge his death; for redemption in the next life, if not this one."

"Menawa is correct, Marco," Coachman said. "I will tell Colonel Coffee that we intend to avoid Fort Gibson entirely, and ask to be let off twenty miles downriver." He pulled a map from his saddle bag. "We will make our way from the Three Forks landing to the Canadian River here, and wait for the rest of the expedition. We were going to explore this river anyway, so nothing is lost and safety is gained." He dipped his head in respect to the old chief.

The group set out in early September. The leaves were promising autumn, but the sun laughed and baked. They rode north and west with what is now known as the South Canadian River on their left, along an alluvial plain fifty miles wide that stretched more than 200 miles from the Arkansas River to the Cross Timbers. It might have partially been the time of year, but the land presented itself well. The blue stem was still plentiful for grazing, walnuts and hickory nuts were dropping from the trees, and maturing gourds, melons, paw-paws and persimmons were providing ample feed for birds and game. Even the grumpy McCurtain and his Chickasaws had to admit that if you had to be banished, you could do a hell of a lot worse.

Marco pegged his ponies near the Army horses and mules at night, took notes and listened. He found that the campfire talk by the engineers was honest, if a bit optimistic. They saw dams where only streams trickled, and bridges for non-existent highways, but Marco understood that was their job; and they were the first to note that the Deep Fork River, although shown as navigable on the maps, was really a maze of sandbanks and shoals that couldn't be trusted.

City boy Marco felt from time to time like he had wandered into an arcade. Even though he was still at best an average shot, he took down two wild turkeys in a single morning, which he presented to a laughing John Coachman like a terrier dropping its kill at the feet of its master.

On another day, he spied a brown bear crashing in fear through the scrub oaks and raised his rifle.

"Don't shoot, Horse Talker," George Gaines said, as he brought his mount close to Marco. "Choctaws won't eat bear and there is no sense shooting what you don't eat. A dead bear is bad luck to the Choctaws."

"Lucky we don't have any Comanches with us,"

Sergeant Blackstock said later. "They won't eat deer."

"Creeks won't eat a snake," Marco said. "I learned that."

"And nobody will eat your biscuits, Sarge," Private Ochs said across the ponies. "It's a wonder we don't all starve to death."

After more than a month of wandering through pines and post oaks together, the group split up. The Choctaws and Chickasaws went south as far as the Red River to scout the land Congress had declared was theirs. The Cherokees traveled up the Verdigris to view their lands around what is now Tahlequah. The Seminoles, who had refused to appoint a delegate, turned their backs on the whole affair and sent nobody, nor would they ever.

There was a chill in the air as the Creeks laid one of their last campfires near an unmapped cascading stream that Buck Tom named Wewoka—Tumbling Waters. Marco dutifully drew and recorded the area in the second of his two large journals.

"So what are your thoughts?" John said, offering Menawa one of his last cigars.

Menawa chose his words carefully. "In one respect, this expedition has done its job. I no longer fear coming to this new land. I think it will be good for corn. I think it will be good for cotton. I think it will be good for some of the rutting bucks who will chase their women over these hills."

He held his smoldering cigar horizontally in front of him to indicate he wasn't through talking. "But I think it is not good for me," he said finally. "It is not coming here that occupies my heart, it is leaving home. How can I leave the ponds and streams that my grandfathers fished? The little path behind my house? It has been there a thousand years. I want to stay in my home. I want to grow old and tell winter stories to the little ones, in the very place the stories happened. And when it comes my time, I want to lie down beside my ancestors." He shook his head. "For me, there will be no coming, because there will be no leaving. Those are my thoughts."

When the delegates met again at the Three Forks ferry to return to Fort Smith, the weather had turned bitter cold. Colonel Coffee obtained Army blankets for everyone, including a small cluster of women new to the group.

"Who are these people, Colonel?" George Gaines asked.

"They are a few of the Indians from near the fort." Coffee pointed to a gray-haired woman who had pulled her blanket up to her nose. "That woman speaks English. She told the commander that she and her sisters have sworn off whiskey and now fear for their lives. They want to return with us to Creek country to make a fresh start. Can't say how much of a start it will be, but they will die for certain if they stay here. What do you say?"

At that moment, the gray-haired woman threw off her blanket and ran at Menawa, screaming like a banshee and raising a hunting knife.

If she had been as tall as a man, Menawa might have been killed on the spot. She plunged her knife once, twice, into the old chief's thigh. His horse shied a bit, and she never got a third try. Sergeant Blackledge shot her full in the chest with his Colt service revolver, sending her flying back into the panicked and crying other women. Lighthorseman Buck Tom quickly joined the sergeant, his rifle pointed at the women. "The next one of you who moves is dead," he said in Creek.

Marco was the first to get to the slumping chief, and pulled him gently to the ground, using his own blanket to cover Menawa. "Are you badly hurt?" Marco asked.

The old chief seemed at peace. "I am dead, as I told you before. Maybe not today, but soon." Coachman kneeled down and Menawa reached for his arm. "Co-cha-ma, take me home. I want to die in my little cabin."

Chapter Nine

The assailant's knife had deeply sliced the old chief's brittle femur, and it snapped as they carried him to the ferry.

Colonel Coffee secured a stretcher from the Fort Smith sick bay, but there was no doctor available. The post's medic bandaged Menawa as well as he could and everyone hoped for the best.

At first Menawa seemed to be recovering. His appetite, especially for beef and corn bread, returned. He spent his days on the riverboat on a chaise in the dining room, telling Marco and Buck Tom about the old days in Alabama, where the turkeys were fatter, the deer more plentiful, the pines loftier than anything they had encountered in the western lands. He was good-natured about it, telling his stories like fables about a magical time that would never return.

By the time they got to the fort doctor in Memphis, however, Menawa had a fever and one of the spots where he had been stabbed was fiery red.

"His wound has putrefied," the Army surgeon said. "I've covered it with sulfa powder and we will watch him for a day or two. But it may be too late. I may have to amputate."

Menawa asked quietly, "What is he saying, Co-cha-ma? I don't understand those words."

John Coachman tried to be as matter-of-fact as possible. "He says your leg does not look good, and in order to save you, he may have to cut it off."

Menawa grasped Coachman's sleeve again. "Please, Co-cha-ma, take me home now. I do not want to go into the next world on one leg. Do you hear me? Will you honor me? Will you take me home?"

"Of course I will, old friend."

Colonel Coffee came to Marco as he was tending the horses. "Young fellow, tell Mr. Coachman that I suggest you remove the old man as soon as possible, tonight if you can. If that old man stays here, they will cut off his leg for sure. That's what Army surgeons do. They'll cut off your leg for a toothache. When I told the surgeon that the chief wanted to keep his leg, he said no offense, but since when does a savage know more about medicine than a doctor?"

Marco went to John Coachman immediately to relay the message.

"This presents a bit of a problem. Menawa can't sit a horse, and a buckboard would kill him sure as the world. We have little time. Come with me, we'll go to the stockyards where we sold our ponies last summer. We need to buy a conveyance that will keep him alive while we move him." He blew out a breath of resignation. "At least until we can bring him home."

They settled on a double buggy with side-wheel suspension, as comfortable as a nineteenth century wagon was likely to get. They bundled the old chief in half a dozen blankets to protect him against the December cold, and left in the dead of night. Coachman asked Marco to drive. He then asked Buck Tom to go alone to Sunrise Farm and tell his mother that they would be delayed as they took the southern route to Alabama and Menawa's home in Okfuskee Town.

They went south along the big river to avoid any snow, then set out east along the Tallahatchie River into Creek country. They hit rain here and there, but that proved to be a benefit of sorts. The mud softened the ruts.

With John Coachman leading, Marco handled the reins of the surprisingly smooth buggy. Marco had driven any number of wagons at the stable, some with teams of two and four. He could handle this one-horse rig in his sleep, and occasionally did.

Menawa was silent and appeared to sleep the first night and day, stirring only to take soup from Coachman's bowl. On the second morning he spoke to

Marco, startling the young man's daydreams.

"I hear you are becoming one of the People," Menawa said, using the Creek word for "Creek." "That is a good thing. Would you like to hear a story of how we People became the People? This mud is part of it."

"Very much," Marco said in surprise, his reverie broken.

"I do as well, grandfather," Coachman said as he drew his horse alongside. He used the affectionate, but respectful word to indicate that they were now more than friends.

The old man's voice was strong. "Long ago, long before there was time, there was just the earth. The People and all the animals were in it, but couldn't move. They asked Ibofango for help, and he sent the rain. Now there was much water. But it was his first time and he sent too much. So now the People and animals were in mud and could move about, but could not see or hear and it frightened them. Crawdad said he could lift the People up out of the mud, but he was just bragging as usual. Finally, the big Turtle, bigger than all this," he motioned with a sweeping gesture, "told the People 'I know earth and I know water. Get on my back and I will take you out of the mud and above the water and I will become Turtle Island and that is where the People will live.'" Menawa paused to take a breath.

"That is a wonderful story, Micco," Marco said, using the even more respectful term for chief.

Menawa coughed up a laugh. "Just like every colt. Ready to run. Be patient, my near-People friend. That is only half the story. I will sleep on it and then tell you the rest."

The next day, as they neared Tupelo, Menawa emerged from his cocoon, startling Marco once again. The old man laughed. "Runs like a colt, jumps like a cricket. Are you ready to hear more about the first People?"

"Yes, please."

The chief stared into the distance the way storytellers do. "Things did not go well on Turtle Island. So many of us all together on the island made it hot and, with so much water, the island became covered in fog. The People still could not see and were ignorant. So Ibofango sent the Master of Breath to blow a gentle breeze from the east to get rid of the fog. The Master of Breath did as he was told, but to show his power he also sent silly winds, dirt devils from the south, and from time to time, mean winds like tornadoes down from the north. Finally the fog was blown into the dark corners of the west, and all the People and every animal could see each other and understand our place in the world."

"Is that the end of the story?" Marco asked, more cautiously than before.

"Far from it, Horse Talker. With no fog, there was a great brightness that blazed too hot and caused pain among the People and the animals. There was much discussion among everyone whether to live in the brightness where it is hot and shiny, or in the darkness where it is cold. The bat said dark, because he hunted best in the dark. The bear agreed, because he liked to sleep. The snake said sun brightness, so he could be happy and warm. But the wise deer said there are advantages to both, so the owl and bat can still hunt, and the snake and butterfly can warm themselves, and the People can sleep and work in turn. Ibofango said, 'That is wise, and it will be done, but I am tired now and need my rest.'"

Menawa paused, then groaned.

"That is enough for now, grandfather," Coachman said. "Your lessons for Horse Talker are important, and I am learning much myself, but even Ibofango needed rest. You said so yourself. Rest a while."

Off and on for the next few days, Menawa told Marco stories of how Grandfather Sun and Grandmother Moon were created and how the raccoon's tail was used to tell the passing from bright to dark, thus creating time.

Late one evening, with a small campfire sputtering, Coachman approached the bundle of blankets that was Menawa at rest. "I've got some stew, grandfather, with some rabbit to make you tricky. We are almost home now. Try to eat a bite and then perhaps you can tell Horse Talker another story, maybe how the stars got in the skies."

Marco touched the old chief's arm and a blanket dropped away from his sightless eyes. "Sweet Jesus," Marco said in English. "He's dead, Mister Coachman, he's dead."

"Well, I am sad, but not surprised," Coachman said with a sigh. "He lasted as long as he could, and it almost got him home. I think telling you the creation stories kept him alive. His journey is over, but ours is not. I know you won't fully understand what I say, but we will find a thousand-year-old path and bury him with his ancestors. We reach Okfuskee Town tomorrow."

Chapter Ten

The two men would have reached Okfuskee Town, but Okfuskee Town was gone.

It had been burned to the ground—every little cabin, the meeting house, the corn cribs, even the nearby trees and stubbly corn fields. And there wasn't a trace of the people who once lived in the village. Just ashes.

John Coachman shook involuntarily. "I am glad Menawa didn't live to see this," he said. "I almost wish I hadn't."

"I don't understand," Marco said. "There was a town here?"

"Yes, an Indian town, like Hope Town," Coachman answered. "I was only here once, but it was pretty big for Creeks, maybe fifty or sixty cabins. But it didn't just burn down, I'm thinking. Look to your right, at that building on the hill. That's a white man's building, probably a trading post. It wasn't here before and it's not supposed to be here now. Follow me."

They crested the hill to find not one, but three substantial buildings and a landing for a ferry. At their approach, a heavyset man came out of the door of the main building, leaned his rifle against the door jamb, and threw open his arms in greeting.

"Welcome, stranger, welcome. Welcome to Enright's Tavern and Mercantile Store. I can tell by your fancy rig and the cut of your cloth that you are a gentleman of quality. Come in and have a look around, have a sip of some of the finest bourbon this side of Kentucky." He paused a beat. "You'll have to leave your boy outside, of course."

John Coachman leaned forward in his saddle. "Since when does a white man sell whiskey to an Indian? You bootlegging in addition to trespassing?"

The man went pale. "You're an Injun? Where did you get that buggy and them clothes?"

Coachman sat bolt upright. "I am a proud member of the Creek Nation with every right to be here. You, on the other hand, are in violation of state and federal law. You are probably too dumb to read and write, so I'll tell you that the Treaty of Dancing Rabbit Shoals says no white man may live, work or in any way use this land along the Chattahoochee. This is Creek land. Did you set that fire, you scoundrel?"

The man had dropped his arms by this time. He started moving slowly toward the door where his rifle rested. "Hell, no, I didn't set no fire. I heard there was a fire a while back...."

Coachman quickly pulled his own rifle from its scabbard and pointed it directly at the tavern owner. "If you take another step I will blow a hole in you as big as your fist. I sort of wish you'd try."

Shaken, the man moved away from his gun. "You can't do that. An Injun kills a white man, he'll be dancing at the end of a rope in Mobile." His voice grew more confident as he spoke.

"And you will be just as dead," Coachman said evenly. "You are trespassing and you know it. When I come back here in three days, you had best be gone. And it won't be just me rousting you out; I will have the soldiers from Fort Mitchell with me."

Coachman wheeled and trotted close to his young companion in the buggy. In a low voice he said, "Get that curious look off your face, Marco. We are not returning. I'm hoping the threat of soldiers will send him packing, but I have no illusions. Head north along the river. I'll keep an eye on this scalawag until you are out of sight."

That night they reached Cuto Town, a rough little village ten miles from the river near a granite outcropping. The people there had heard of Co-cha-ma, of course, and welcomed Coachman and Marco into the community house for a meal of sofki and corn bread. The group of people in the building was large and agitated, peppering the two travelers with questions in a manner that at another time might seem un-Indian. Coachman and Marco soon learned that many in the building were dispossessed residents of Okfuskee Town.

"When will Menawa return?" asked one man in a gray striped blanket. "He will lead us back to rebuild our town. Weren't you together exploring the new land? Why aren't you together now?"

"My friends," Coachman said, clearing his throat. "I bring you the sad news that the great Menawa died on the trail a few days ago." There was immediate wailing and moaning unlike anything Marco had heard before. Coachman waited for the noise to die down before he continued. "I have brought him here to be buried in the proper Creek way. I will ask a few of you to join me in sitting with him."

"But what will become of us now?" asked another man Coachman recognized as Eco Hutkay—White Deer. "The people of Cuto Town are very generous, but we are many, and we have nothing. Nothing. Our corn is gone. And where shall we plant for next year? Will the white man chase us away again? And what shall we eat for six moons until the corn is high? We will starve to death and pull these generous people to their deaths behind us. We are lost, I think."

John Coachman gave a response so spontaneous, so opposite of what he once felt, it surprised even him. "My people, I agree, and Menawa agreed, that your future here is clouded. It takes a year to harvest and store enough corn to take you and your children through the winter. But it takes only one fiery night to destroy it. The white man knows this as well as you. He will never leave you in peace. You know this."

The words came tumbling out of Coachman's mouth with a resolve the people needed to hear. "You have a future, but it is not here. Chief Menawa and I agreed that the land offered by the federal government is good land—good for corn, good for cotton, good for you. Certainly, it will not be easy. In fact, it will be hard. But the land will be yours and yours alone, no white man behind every rock and tree." He nodded for emphasis. "You must leave. You must leave and not look back."

White Deer seemed annoyed. "Words of advice are always fearless. But leave where? Leave how? Our wagons were burned and our horses were taken."

Coachman remained calm. "You must follow the river to Mobile. The Army is waiting for you there. They will give you food and clothing, then transport you by boat to your new land."

White Deer persisted. "Will you lead us? Will you take us there?"

Coachman hesitated, because his natural inclination was to do just that. But his obligation to his own clan was overpowering. "I regret that I cannot, Eco Hutkay. I have hundreds of families just like yours, waiting for my return. But I will do what I can. I will send my friend Horse Talker ahead while I sit with Menawa. In four days' time he will return with three wagons and as much clothing as we can spare. Meanwhile you must prepare yourselves. And help me find a place for Menawa's passage."

He spoke quietly to Marco. "Take the buggy to Sunrise and tell Uncle Hes-se to send three wagons here straight away. Ask Mother to find as many blankets and food as we can spare. I don't know how she does it, but she and Aunt Rabbit always seem to find a way."

Marco approached a Hope Town twice as large as the one he had left six months earlier. The new cabins were poorly built, some barely more than lean-tos. The tidy sense of order that had so impressed Marco had been replaced by a more chaotic group of strangers. The smoke from a dozen little campfires betrayed the fact that this was an encampment now, not a town. New Town had not burned like Okfuskee, but the community was gone nevertheless.

Confused and wary, Marco stopped the buggy and called into the afternoon shadows. "*Hensci, hensci,* greeting, greetings," he yelled. "Haya-Atke? Uncle Hes-se? Halloo?"

Haya-Atke came flying out of the old house, her

salt-and-pepper hair uncharacteristically unbraided, giving her an unkempt, almost threatening visage. She leaned into the buggy and began patting Marco tenderly on his arms and chest.

"Oh, Marco, you have returned!" she shouted with joy. Her eyes darted. "Where is my son? Is he all right? Is he coming?"

"He is fine, Grandmother, he is fine. He has been delayed, but he will be here in two days." Marco's demeanor became very serious. "His old friend, Chief Menawa, died. Mr. Coachman is in Cuto Town to bury him."

Haya-Atke sucked air through her clenched teeth, then cocked her head. "But why Cuto Town? Menawa was chief of Okfuskee Town. He should be buried there."

Marco looked at his hands, avoiding eye contact. "Okfuskee Town is no more, Grandmother. Some white men burned it to the ground. They burned all the corn cribs, too, and chased the people into the woods. We saw many of the Okfuskee in Cuto Town. It was very sad."

She patted his arm again. "We are no stranger to sadness here, as well," she said. "My son will restore order, but you have been gone a very long time, and the world has changed." She climbed into the buggy and drew a blanket over their legs. "And this changed world has taught me that I have much to learn, Marco.

Do you remember when I told you that there were no Indian orphanages, that it was a white man's curse?"

"Of course I do."

"We find ourselves with a similar need for the first time. So many of our people are dying—dying in jails, dying of sickness, dying of starvation, being chased like animals. And you might think that children, being small, would die first, but it is just the opposite. The desire to live is very strong among the young." She laughed. "The clans are overwhelmed. And because Hope Town is safe and we still have food, an army of children has made its way here."

"Where are you keeping them?"

"Oh, they are here, we will get to that. But Marco, I knew nothing of running an orphanage, so—please forgive me—I wrote to your Sisters of Carondelet in Cincinnati, asking for advice. I didn't know where else to turn."

Marco was actually proud, and curious. "Could the Sisters provide you any assistance?"

"In abundance. Please, take me to the big house. I want to show you something."

Marco drove them through the apple trees, and as they rounded the stables, he saw dozens of children on the sprawling front porch of the plantation-style big house. Standing in their center was Sister Irene.

Chapter Eleven

It took Marco a second to recognize her. To say she was the last person on Earth he expected wasn't much of a stretch. In addition, her habit had been softened to make her appear more approachable, more motherly. Her black robe had been replaced with a gray tunic and white apron, a simple white coif and white veil. She looked more like a nurse than a nun, which was exactly the point.

Sister Irene was the closest thing to a mother Marco had ever had, and he enthusiastically and unconsciously bounded up the steps of the porch to embrace her.

"Oh, my dear Lord." She giggled. The children giggled, too, simply because they liked to giggle. "What would your classmates at St. Matt's think of you hugging a nun? Oh, well, *mundi praepostere*. It's a topsy-turvy world. I'm so pleased to see you, too, Marco." She held him at arm's length to take him in. "Look at you. A man in full. Amazing what a year will do."

"Yes, Sister," Marco answered proudly. "I am a full-fledged Indian now." He repeated it in Creek.

Sister Irene put her hand to her mouth in surprise. "Your fluency astonishes me. Thank goodness for that, because this language perplexes me. The little ones don't mind, of course. As long as I pat their heads and fill their little bellies, they are robust balls of mirth." She paused. "It moves me that God made all babies so amused at everything, even their toes. I think a child's laughter is the voice of our Father."

She busied herself with a towel. "All right, end of sermon. But you know children. Some of the older ones are filled with curiosity about this stranger in their midst. They talk, they question; for all I know, perhaps they tease me just a little. You can help me by talking with the children."

Marco laughed. "That sounds like a good job for me. Some of the Creeks here, like Uncle Hes-se, think that I sound like a child myself. I should fit right in. Pretty soon I will be able to talk to babies as well as horses."

"Horses?"

Again Marco laughed. "It's a gift, I guess. I think Mr. Coachman and the other Indians saw it in me before I did, that I am very good with horses, Sister. The name they gave me in the Creek language is Horse Talker, Iyabi-Corakko. I'm Mr. Coachman's wrangler now."

Sister Irene's eyebrows rose in maternal pride. "Wrangler? I know what *that* means. Brother Bartholomew will be very proud, Marco. He gave me a letter for you and another for John Coachman. Did he arrive with you?"

"No, Sister, he remained behind to bury a friend we lost returning from the Western lands. He'll be along in a few days."

Irene sighed. "I will actually be grateful for the timing, then, dear boy. Perhaps you can intervene on my behalf and explain how we turned his beautiful plantation into a citadel for lost children."

Marco's mien became serious. "He will understand *how*; he and I saw an entire village burned to the ground, scattering men and women like chaff. But it will be far harder for him, and me, to understand the evil *why*—why white men feel free to steal, burn out, even kill the Indian. Have white churches in Alabama closed? Has God turned a blind eye on the South?"

Irene patted his hand. "These are legitimate questions, Marco. I, too, have asked them. That is one of the reasons I came. I wanted to see with my own eyes that which my heart could not fathom." She swung her arm wide over the porch and smiled. "But that wasn't the main reason I came. I came to hear giggling babies."

*   *   *

The next morning Marco headed south along the river road with a fresh pony in tow in order to welcome his mentor, John Coachman. He figured that the steadfast and gallant Amber King would be dead tired by now and wanted to give Coachman's horse a breather. He needn't have worried—the muddied but proud horse came up the road like it was leading a parade. The big mount rarely bothered to trot; it went right from walk to prance, often on the oblique.

"Hail, Marco!" Coachman shouted. "Tell me, my friend. What news of Sunrise Farm? How is my mother? How is the village?"

"Your mother is well, and the farm is thriving." Marco fell into pace with Coachman. "In fact, some would say teeming." He spent the next few minutes explaining how Hope Town had become a refugee center, how Coachman's plantation house had been turned into an orphanage, and finally, about the arrival of Sister Irene.

"This pleases me," Coachman said. "The house was too big for me anyway, and Mother would not set foot in it. Now that it is full of Creek children, perhaps her feelings have softened. And I'm glad Sister Irene is here. She was the spunky one, yes? I think Brother Bartholomew was smitten, not to mention intimidated by her."

"Sister brought a letter from Brother Bartholomew for you," Marco said. He paused and looked into the bare trees. "Smitten. So that's why Brother Bart was so steadfast. Back in the days when I was only a white man, that flew right by me." They both laughed.

Brother Bartholomew's letter to Marco had been chatty and familial, a proud uncle writing to his favorite nephew. He brought Marco up to date on some of his schoolmates, and told him that Mickey was now his apprentice. "He is gradually catching on," Bart wrote generously, which Marco understood to mean that he was struggling. Bart was full of praise for Marco's venture into the western lands. "The whole world now knows of your adventures. Sister Irene tells me that the *New York Tribune* mentioned you by name as 'a member of the Indian delegation'—they used those very words—sent to explore the new Indian territories. I hope you found it suitable, Marco, because Sister Irene says that President Jackson has told the newspapers that in one year you will go there, either on your own or at the point of a bayonet. I am proud of her for helping to make ready your journey and proud of you for trailblazing. I remain your friend and your champion, Brother Bartholomew."

Bart's letter to John Coachman was equally friendly, but much darker.

"My dear Mister Coachman, I commend into your hands my friend, the caring, brave and headstrong

Sister Irene. She believes that she has been called to 'suffer the little children,' as it says in the Bible, and I applaud her efforts as well as fear for her safety.

"My purpose in writing you this letter is to relate to you things I have seen and heard, things that Sister Irene may be too polite to tell you. In October, when you and Marco were exploring the western territory, I took my blacksmithing to Lexington as usual for the fall horse auction. I noticed, though not at first, that there were no Indian traders to be seen. I asked Mr. Compton, the auction overseer, about that and he said Kentucky law now forbids Indians from selling their horses at auction, or even obtaining a bid number to buy. He said similar laws had been passed in Tennessee, Georgia, the Carolinas and Alabama. I said that seemed unduly harsh, but he said not when you consider that in less than two years, there will not be a single Indian living east of the Mississippi. They are leaving, and they will be leaving their horses behind. He said that, in a way, keeping them out of the auctions is a kindness. At least this prevents Indians from trading for horses they cannot keep.

"This kind of thinking is a travesty and unholy, but it is pervasive. Sister Irene says that President Jackson is in league with the Devil, ordering Indians banished from their homes 'to protect them and give them a land all their own.' It is true that the Indian needs protection, sir, but it is from the very militias and local constabularies established to serve us all. And Sister says that when an Indian finally can no longer take it and fights back, he is killed and the newspapers are filled with stories of 'Indian uprisings.'

"Mr. Coachman, I understand your belief that landed Indians are safe from removal. But I fear that belief is unfounded. There is little I can do to help, but Sister Irene says we must do something. So I propose that come spring, when it is time to sell the yearlings, you drive your ponies here to Cincinnati, and Marco and I will drive them the rest of the way to Saratoga for auction. To make everything legal, you can sell your horses to the Sisters, who will then become owners of record. I urge you to sell your stock, sir, before it is wrested from you.

"I remain your faithful friend, Brother Bartholomew."

That evening, a concerned John Coachman convened with his mother, Marco, and Sister Irene. "Odd, isn't it?" he said. "Here we are in the heart of Indian country, but the Indians seem to be the last to know of our situation. George Gaines and I talked about this. George told me the Cherokees are suffering, but they would never seek help from us Creeks, even if we could provide it, out of pride and thousand-year-old suspicions. The Choctaws are leery of the Cherokees for much the same reasons, and nobody seems to know what the Seminoles are doing in Florida. We tell each other that we have men in Washington who will help us, that things will get better, but we are guessing. Are we playing the fool? Sister Irene, it may seem illogical that a nun in Cincinnati should know more about our condition than we ourselves, but I am sure the newspapers in Cincinnati, Cleveland and New York are better informed, and vastly more truthful, than those in Atlanta, Mobile and Montgomery. Please speak plainly, Sister. Is our plight as serious as Brother Bartholomew paints it?"

Sister was silent for a moment, looking at the floor. Then she lifted her head and returned Coachman's gaze. "God forgive me, but in some places like Georgia, it is worse. It's all about the land, of course. Men join the Georgia militia, it is said, just to drive away Indians and take their land as their own. And, according to the *New York Tribune*'s reporter in Atlanta, there are far more militiamen in Georgia than federal troops, so Andrew Jackson gleefully says he can do nothing, the Georgia people have spoken."

"It is just as bad here," Haya-Atke said. "When Uncle Hes-se brought his wagon back from Mobile, he said the city itself was safe, filled with soldiers at the docks loading the people into steamboats. But he said the Chattahoochee was now more than just a river. It was a 200-mile gauntlet with treacherous white men on every side, ready to steal, ready to rape, ready to kill. He said if it hadn't been for the soldiers at Fort Mitchell, he and his cargo of women and children might not have made it through."

"We saw in Okfuskee Town what happens when the soldiers are elsewhere, didn't we, Marco?" Coachman said quietly.

"Even that small amount of protection may end soon," said Irene. "The Mobile newspaper says that Jackson is threatening to withdraw all federal troops from Fort Mitchell. He says it is no longer in the country's best interest to garrison hundreds of American soldiers just to protect a smattering of uneducated, ungrateful and undisciplined savages."

John Coachman put his elbows on the dining table, his chin in his hands. "Fort Mitchell is our way station on the long trek to Mobile. The soldiers there are generous and friendly, giving our people food, water and the occasional blanket. If that is gone, our people will walk cold and hungry right into an enemy camp. We are told we must leave, yet without a way station to care for the sick and elderly, and to provide a little food for the children, many of our people won't make it to the boats, much less the western lands."

The room was silent for long seconds. Then Sister Irene stood. "Mister Coachman, with your help and the grace of God, I would like to be that way station."

Chapter Twelve

Sister Irene, née Irene Rippy, was the last of seven children born to Irish immigrants in New York City. As often happened in poor Catholic families at the time, she was sent off to be a nun, as a gift to the church and one less mouth to feed at home. Still a teenager when she entered the order, she developed two traits that didn't serve her particularly well. First, she became, through no fault of her own, pretty. This made her not quite unpopular, but marginalized and subject to suspicion from some church higher-ups. Next she developed an intelligence filled with curiosity. She questioned things other nuns didn't and got sent to Manila as a nurses' aide for her impertinence. She returned four years later, recovered from malaria, a nurse in her own right; pretty, curious and still unable to hold her tongue.

Irene was good for the St. Matthew's orphanage, her sass and savvy making her very popular with the boys, even the older ones whose desire to break free included breaking free from the church. She was right for the orphanage, but it was too small to contain her forever. The reverend Mother Cornelia, who adored Irene, once said that in time Irene would have to be "repotted." That's why when she received Haya-Atke's letter, she actually felt relief.

Mother Cornelia gave her permission at once. It was ideal: Sister Irene would be doing the Lord's work ministering to the innocent and needy babies of the lost tribes of Israel, she would be her own boss, and the assignment would be for only three years. The Indians would all be gone by then, living on the dark side of the moon across the Mississippi River. Irene would return to St. Matthew's more mature and ready to help ease Mother Cornelia into retirement. Perhaps to even succeed her.

By the summer of 1833, another six months had passed. Sunrise Farm had become the site of an uneasy peace between Sister Irene and John Coachman.

Coachman was accustomed to giving orders. Sister Irene was comfortable ignoring them if they clashed with her worldview. Their mutual respect kept the lid on things.

He found her mid-morning, as usual, on the porch of the old house. She was finishing up her daily English instruction. Also as usual, the porch was populated almost entirely by women, with the prideful but curious men standing or sitting nearby, pretending to work. They scattered when they saw Co-cha-ma approach.

"Sorry to break up your classes, Sister. And I thank you for your kindness. But you see, how can I possibly let you go?" He sat down on a cane back chair previously occupied by one of the scattered students. "I admire your desire to help my people, you must know that. You have done wonders here," Co-cha-ma said. "But leaving, no matter how well intended, would mean abandoning your children, your instructions, everything here. You've turned despair into hope for the little ones; a hope, frankly, that feeds us all. I myself have seldom felt so in the moment, unafraid to face a future laced with uncertainty."

"I am not proposing to leave tomorrow. And I have been training a cadre of nursing staff before I go," Sister Irene replied evenly. "Sadly, your future is not laced with uncertainty. It is stitched tight with the dreadful certainty that every one of your people, everyone including you, will be forced to emigrate to the western lands, either on your own or escorted by soldiers."

"I am half white, remember, and owner of one of the most successful horse farms in Tennessee," Coachman said with a hint of heat.

"Perhaps Andrew Jackson will banish only the

Indian half of you," she responded a bit too quickly. She paused and blew out a tiny puff of air. "Oh dear, that came out wrong for both of us, didn't it? Please forgive me. I meant no disrespect."

"Nor did I," Coachman said. "But it is odd, isn't it? I think of Marco, who desires to live as an Indian. My nation says welcome, while the federal government says good riddance. But because my mother is Creek, the government calls me a half-breed, whatever that means, and threatens me with removal. Even if my mother and father were white and my grandmother was Indian, I would still be an Indian in the eyes of the federals. And here is a very crazy thing: if both my parents were white, both my grandparents were white and my poor old great-grandmother were Creek, the Creeks would say I'm white, but the whites would still say I'm Indian. I'm proud to be an Indian, Sister, but the whole bloodline business stupefies me."

Irene nodded. "I've read that among the slaves, if you have any negro blood at all, you are considered a negro. It's called the 'one drop rule.' It seems that whites, especially Southern whites, have forgotten that God loves us all and expects us to love one another."

Coachman smiled broadly. "I am glad you are here to remind us. My 'love' for the men who burned down Okfuskee Town was wearing passing thin. But to get back to the matters at hand, there is much to be discussed. You and I disagree on the forced emigration of my people, that is true. I believe it is Jackson's bravado, not his resolve. But I am a practical man. If I am wrong, people will die; if you are wrong, life will go on here just as before, knee-deep in laughing babies. God may love us, but doesn't it also say that God helps those who help themselves?"

He rested his elbows on his knees and bent forward in his seat. "I agree that preparations must be made. How can we help?"

"I've been studying what to do. We are not allowed to go inside Fort Mitchell, but we can set up as near as practical. You and I know that the soldiers have absolutely nothing to do, protecting Alabamans against nonexistent 'Indian uprisings.' And the very presence of a Federal Army fort filled with mostly Northern soldiers will dissuade white vigilantes from bothering us."

Though she sat beside Coachman she talked to the orchard, avoiding eye contact. "My supposition, taken from the newspaper reports, is that the people we will encounter at this station will be poorer, sicker, hungrier and more confused than the refugees we are seeing here. I have read that the Army has field hospitals, large tents set up to provide first aid, medicines and surgery. We won't be providing surgery, of course, but the tents would be a Godsend, providing shelter for the little ones, a bit of food and a place to rest and recover. And as you noted earlier, give a glimmer of hope in the darkness. Can I get one of them?"

"I doubt that *you* can, but I may be able to. Next month Marco and I will drive our horses to Cincinnati, where Brother Bart will shoe them so they don't look like Indian ponies. Then while he and Marco take them to Saratoga for sale, I will go to Washington and talk to the War Office. I will speak to Secretary Cass; he already thinks I'm a chief because I was a member of the delegation sent to explore the land west of the Mississippi. I will remind him that just as he hoped, I am now preparing to move my people to Mobile for riverboat passage to the new territory." He grinned. "I will mention that your New York newspapers are interested in sending journalists along to report on the emigration, and I would prefer getting my people to Mobile alive. Cass will give me a tent city just to get rid of me."

Chapter Thirteen

Marco returned to St. Matt's with a mixture of anticipation and trepidation.

He felt that he was an entirely different person than the idealistic boy who left almost two years prior. He was a man, a wrangler, a horse talker, an Indian. But would St. Matt's have changed as well, or just grown a few years older?

Driving his ponies into the Carondelet stables, he got his answer soon enough. Brother Bartholomew was exactly the same sinewy little man, only Marco was now a head taller. This amused both of them.

They slapped each other on the shoulders. Once again Marco was reminded of his former boss's strength. "Well, Lord love you, son, you've shot up like a weed. That Indian food must hit the spot. What do they feed you down there?"

"Mostly steaks and caviar, Brother Bart. Doesn't taste half bad if you wash it down with enough fine champagne."

Bart laughed heartily. "Glad to see when they put

the Indian in you, they didn't take the imp out. I always liked that little imp. *Big* imp, forgive me. Speaking of growing, I got an old friend of yours around here somewhere." He turned and yelled, "Hey Mickey, quit napping behind those bales and come meet your old classmate."

A thick-bodied man-child came lumbering out of a distant stall. Marco stared. The shock of red hair was the same, but Mickey's beefy face had grown sullen.

"Well, if it ain't Cincinnati's favorite Injun. Welcome back. Just in time, too. I can always use an assistant mucker." He made no attempt to approach Marco, preferring to stay a few paces behind Brother Bart.

"Hi, Mickey," Marco replied brightly. "Brother Bartholomew has written me that you are coming along just fine as his new apprentice." He cut his eyes toward Bart at his half-truth.

"Yeah, well, thanks a lot for not warning me," Mickey said. "This is the hardest damn job in the orphanage. You're out going 'woo, woo, woo' all over the place and I'm stuck here shoveling horse manure. You might have said something."

Brother Bart patted Mickey gently on the shoulder. "I swear, Mick, you're going to give yourself the vapors complaining about yesterday's sunset. It was a good job when Marco had it; it's a good job now. When I was a boxer we used to say roll with the punch. It's still good advice." He turned back to Marco. "So where's your boss, Mr. Coachman?"

"Over at the orphanage with the Reverend Mother signing bills of transfer to the Sisters. By the end of the day Mother Cornelia will have a string of ponies that will make her the envy of every man in Cincinnati. If we keep this up, maybe I should come back as *her* wrangler."

"You could do worse, my friend. I find it most appealing," said Brother Bart. "Well, let's make the new owners proud. These ponies won't shoe themselves." He patted the withers of a young paint. "Let's start with this delicate filly. Mick, fetch me the flat head foal nipper. Don't want to spook her."

Mickey approached a table arrayed with nippers, shoe pullers and clinchers like it was filled with snakes. He stared, frozen in almost comical confusion. In a gesture of camaraderie, Marco picked up the foal nipper and offered it to Mickey. "I think this is what Brother Bart is looking for."

Mickey snatched the nipper and shook it angrily at Marco. His face had turned vermillion. "I knew what it was, I knew what it was, you bastard!" he screamed and hurled the nipper into a vacant stall. "Go get it, Injun bastard!" he yelled again, then whirled and ran out of the stable.

"What did I do?" asked a mystified Marco.

"Nothing. It's not your fault, son. He's done it

before. He's usually back for supper. It is partly my doing, I'm afraid. Sometimes I am short of temper with him. And even when I say nothing, he can see disappointment in my eyes. It's not entirely his fault, either. He's a simple lad who has gone as far as he can go. This makes him angry at you, at me, at the Sisters, at a world that perplexes him. You are a hard act to follow, as they say." He rubbed his gnarly hands together. "Well, it's back to the Bart and Marco main event. Just like the old days. We have a dozen ponies to shoe before we head out at first light tomorrow."

Bart paused and lowered his voice just above a whisper. "And this is a case where two is probably more than three."

John Coachman arrived at the Georgetown home of Thomas Grayson, a white man who was legal counsel for the Creek nation. Just like John's father, Grayson had married a Creek woman, Idabel. The Grayson home sat on a hill above Rock Creek and was less than two miles from the offices of the secretary of war. Grayson was a trusted family friend and greeted Coachman like a long lost relative.

"At last, somebody in the Capitol who speaks the truth. Welcome, dear friend, come in, come in. My wife has concocted an elixir to refresh the weary traveler, otherwise known as lemonade. It awaits us on the south porch."

John gratefully dropped his carpetbag near the door and sank into one of the nearly-ubiquitous white wicker chairs that announced a Southern lifestyle. A humorist at the *New York Post* at the time wrote that Washington was a Southern island surrounded by a sea of Yankees. It remains more or less the same to this day.

Grayson offered Coachman a cigar, and they settled into the time-honored male conversational stance of looking everywhere except at each other.

Grayson blew a puff of smoke toward Rock Creek. "When your letter reached me last week, it seemed a bit shy of specifics. As delighted as I am to see you, I hope you haven't come to Washington to renew our efforts to avoid emigration. I'm afraid Congressional intent has congealed around that issue."

"No, my friend. I am here, believe it or not, to beg a tent or two from the Army. I represent some, uh, nursing friends who intend to set up a field hospital and way station near Fort Mitchell in Alabama. Many many of my people are emigrating down the Chattahoochee to Mobile for riverboat passage to the western lands. They are so terrified of what is behind them, they are willing to accept the uncertainties ahead. And what is behind them is truly evil, Thomas. Men who claim to be God-fearing are pillaging, raping, burning, even killing Indian men and women with impunity. My own farm is testament to this horror; it has become an orphanage for more than a hundred lost and lonely children. I have seen with my own eyes an entire Creek village burned to the ground. Burned to ashes, with the villagers hiding cold and hungry in the woods."

"I have read of such atrocities among the Cherokees in Georgia," Grayson said. "Thank God you and your friends are doing something to help. I will help you get to the right people at the War Department. You shouldn't have any trouble getting what you want. You are one of the emissaries who first visited the new Indian lands, so you will hold sway. And while the government won't lift a finger to help you remain here, it will bend over backwards to help you leave. Sad."

John stared into his lemonade. "It is all most perplexing. We are relatively few compared to whites, I understand that. It's a white man's world. But the Indian and the white man have lived in peace for more than a hundred years. Why suddenly are we so loathsome that we must be chased across the Mississippi like vermin? The so-called 'Indian uprisings' are pure fiction and everybody knows it. What have we done?"

"Ask any Southern congressman and he won't give you a straight answer, John. This is what the great English statesman William Penn called a proxy war.

Our country is fraying, my friend, straining at the seams, about to burst. It is all about slavery, of course. But it can't officially be about slavery, so it is about you. The Southern states are building militias to protect their right to own slaves, but they pretend that they are just protecting their womenfolk from the red savages. Many Northern congressmen can see what the South is doing, but fear an all-out conflict. And Andrew Jackson is a slave owner in sheep's clothing. The South would like to enslave you, too, but doesn't have the clout to do so, so by proxy they insist on banishing the Indian. And make no mistake, if this country ever comes to its senses and outlaws slavery, the South will have a template to send the black man across the river, too."

"So you believe our banishment is certain as well, Thomas? As dire as it is for many of my people, I have read and am led to believe that our emigration was voluntary."

Grayson took a long drag on his cigar. "Oh, it still is … for now."

Chapter Fourteen

John Coachman and Marco returned to Sunrise Farm with not one, but two wagons laden with tents, cots, field tables, lister bags, and as many blankets as they could hold. John's friend Thomas was correct; the War Department was delighted to cooperate, and report to the President its efforts in hastening the Creek emigration. The Fort Washington supply master promised Coachman additional wagonloads of supplies "if conditions warrant them."

The two men entered the village like a circus coming to town, with children skipping alongside and behind the wagons and Sister Irene leading the parade with arms raised like a prize fighter. Although it was summer, a couple of blankets started to disappear. Coachman climbed onto the seat of his wagon and, his arm circling the children in his best imitation of a shaman, boomed in Creek, "Do not touch another thing on these wagons. If you disobey, the Old Hag of the Mountains will come into your room and steal your teeth while you sleep." With hoots of laughter, fearing nothing, the playful children scattered.

"*Ave*, John Coachman, *ave*," sang Sister Irene when the wagons came to a stop in front of the mansion-cum-orphanage. "You have returned triumphant, as I knew you would. Is there enough there for our hospital?"

It was Marco's turn to laugh. "With these wagons and the wagons the fort has promised us, there is enough to start your own city, Sister. Brother Bartholomew sends you greetings, I should add."

After a brief inventory of the wagons that was at least partially meant to conceal her blush, Irene led the men and John's mother, who was the de facto micco of the village, into her combination office and classroom. It had once been a parlor, but John had never liked its lace and unused tea service. This was much better.

"We have been doing our part in the weeks you have been away," Irene said. "With the help of you, dear Haya-Atke," she nodded to John's mother, "I have two able assistants, your sister-in-law Rabbit, Mister Coachman, and a young woman called Rain. Rain speaks and writes English, which is a big help to me." She laughed. "I am helpless as a linguist, I'm afraid. Why can't the world just speak Latin and be done with it?"

She continued, "The three of us are practicing

rudimentary nursing skills; no surgery, of course. Rabbit is instructing us in preparing Creek food—my goodness, you people eat a lot of corn—and now we must teach some of the older boys to erect (do they say pitch?) the tents. We should be ready by September, just when we will begin to be needed most."

"Have you received permission from Fort Mitchell to set up your tents nearby?" John asked.

"In a manner of speaking," Irene answered. "I sent the fort commander a letter asking not only permission to encamp nearby, but whether the fort would supply us with provisions, which we would pay for, of course. I received a letter in return saying that since one of the Army's charges was to assure the peaceful migration of Indians to Mobile and on to the western lands, the siting of a way station near the fort seemed appropriate. He wrote, however, that while his orders were to do the Indians no harm, neither was he allowed to provide assistance of any kind. Because of the Chattahoochee there is water in abundance, but the garrison must import its own food, often from as far away as Louisiana, and there is so little to spare, some of his soldiers have planted their own corn at the edge of the fort."

She paused. "Corn. What a curious thing. It's everywhere and nowhere. With sofki and corn bread, it is the basis of your Creek diet. We have plenty here, because you plant your own. But so does everybody else. You can grow corn in your own backyard, and thousands do, I guess. But there is none for sale, at least to the Indians."

"But what about corn meal?" John asked. "That is our major cash crop. I have seen literally miles of Indian cornfields, rivers of corn. Creek villages don't have many things, but you can bet they have a mill."

Haya-Atke, who had remained respectfully quiet, clasped and unclasped her hands. "They stand empty today, my son. To the vigilantes, our corn is no longer a commodity; it is a target. They burn the corn stores, they burn the cribs, they burn the fields. And our people go hungry."

John began to pace in anger. "Starve the belly and the head will die. So that is their game. And I am forced to sell our horses up north because no one will sell us grain here. Is there nobody we can turn to for help against this treachery?"

The room was shrouded in silence. Finally, Marco spoke. "Sister, what about St. Matthew's?"

"What do you mean?"

"The Reverend Mother already buys enough food for sixty hungry boys and—what?—twenty nuns every day. She bargains hard, I know, but the merchants like her, and she pays on time. She could double her purchases and no one would notice. She could even buy all the hay and grain we need for our horses, by increasing inventory at the stable. I know Brother Bart wouldn't mind."

"I like it, Marco," Irene said as she clapped her hands. "I'm sure Mother Cornelia will approve. When she gave me permission to come here, she said she only wished she could do more. This is more. We'll have to alter the Creek diet a bit, I'm afraid, stick to rice and beans rather than corn. They take less room to transport. Still, transportation in any case may be a problem. Cincinnati is two hundred miles away."

"That will not be difficult," John said. "We'll take the provisions and grain by barge down the river and offload below Louisville for the final trip by wagon." He bit off a rueful laugh. "And finding empty wagons is certainly no problem nowadays. We can use the money from the sale of horses to keep the orphanage solvent. I think our way station just got a supply master."

"This is a matter far too important to entrust to a letter. With your indulgence, Mr. Coachman, I will make this petition to the Reverend Mother in person." Irene's face flushed with pleasure. "And it will please me to see the Sisters again," she said, albeit thinking more about stables than sisters.

The Reverend Mother Cornelia's sharp eye spotted the glances and "accidental" meetings between Sister

Irene and Brother Bartholomew. She had seen similar feelings develop between nuns and laymen before, and it always ended in the nun leaving the order, and often the church itself. She knew that in this case, she would lose both Sister Irene and Brother Bart; they could only be together if they left St. Matt's. Mother Cornelia didn't like to think of herself as selfish, but she still held hopes that Irene would succeed her someday, and everyone agreed that Bart was a master blacksmith and stable manager. His like would not soon be seen again, Cornelia believed.

So, convinced that at least on one level she was being supportive as a show of faith, Cornelia threw herself into assisting Irene's mission. She also secretly hoped that keeping Irene and Bart separated might dull their blossoming ardor. And what Cornelia had to offer was both what she did best and what Sister Irene needed the most.

Mother Cornelia was a consummate bargainer and fundraiser. She had to be both in an orphanage that was perpetually underfunded, and in her two decades at St. Matt's she gained a reputation for being sharp but honest. She could also, according to her recently-retired bishop, "charm the birds out of the trees and coins out of purses."

Very early in her efforts to raise money for Sister Irene's way station, Mother Cornelia realized she faced a challenge. Collecting money for homeless waifs was mostly a matter of patience and persistence. Every rich man in Cincinnati could easily picture an orphan child, and the appeal "there but for the grace of God, go I" often found its moral target.

But raising money for Indians was an abstraction. Most wealthy Ohioans knew Indians only through picture books and periodicals, and President Jackson portrayed them as loathsome and dangerous scoundrels who must be banished to protect white women and children. Cornelia needed a sympathetic character, an object of compassion. She stumbled upon that character quite by accident.

Earlier in the year, Cincinnati got its own daily newspaper, the *Enquirer*, and its editor John Hoyt was intent on building a major newspaper that would provide the journalistic bridge between New York and Chicago. He wanted to do local stories that would have regional, even national significance.

But he was sanguine. His meeting with Mother Cornelia stumbled at first. "Reverend Mother, we are well aware of St. Matthew's, and will do what we can to help you and your young charges thrive. Our readers are interested in heartwarming stories of orphans overcoming disadvantages to become productive citizens of Cincinnati. I'm sure you have many of those stories. But Indians? Our readers are confused at best, indifferent at worst. People we have never known, people who are miles and lifetimes separated from us, are leaving us forever. By giving them money, aren't we merely delaying them on their journey to, well, to oblivion?"

"I understand what you say," Mother Cornelia answered evenly. "In the corporeal sense at least, aren't all of us on our personal journey to oblivion? Life is a journey, Mr. Hoyt, and if we are faithful, sometimes a guardian angel comes along to ease our pains, bolster our hopes, lighten our burdens. Such a woman is Cincinnati's very own Sister Irene, currently on leave from St. Matthew's to establish a way station along the Chattahoochee River in Alabama, to help Indian mothers and children make it safely to the Gulf of Mexico and an uncertain future beyond."

John Hoyt leaned forward, tapping his pencil lightly on his desk. "Finally, a positive story about the removal. A local nun travels hundreds of miles to minister to a nation of people she has never met and will never see again? I'd call that a guardian angel, all right. I thought you had lots of stories, Reverend Mother, and this is a beauty. You can count on us."

The next week a front-page article appeared in the *Enquirer* with the headline "The Angel of the Chattahoochee." It ran column one as a weekly series and the story was soon picked up by every major newspaper in the North. The paper also started and promoted the Angel of the Chattahoochee Fund. And money started coming in.

Chapter Fifteen

It didn't snow very often along the Chattahoochee, but the damned wet cold that came creeping down the valley floor could be just as miserable and make you just as sick. It just took a little longer to get to the bone. And longer still to get rid of.

There were early morning frosts on the ground when Sister Irene, Rabbit and Rain got the way station up and running to their satisfaction. It took longer than anticipated, because with the exception of Marco and Uncle Hes-se from time to time, the women did everything themselves. It also got accomplished in stony isolation, with no help from the watchers in the woods. Some of the young Indian men still hanging around the fort looked on curiously, but were skittish and removed.

Finally Rabbit could stand it no more. She approached a young brave who stood his ground, but looked ready to run. "Why do the People shun us?" she asked. "Can't they see we are here to help? Can't they see we have a place to get warm, a place for the old people and children to rest? What is wrong?"

"What is wrong is everything," answered the youth, puffing his chest with a pride he did not feel. "What we see is Army, Army everywhere, Army tents, Army blankets. The micco says beware, the blankets may be poison. He says stay away. It shamed us to beg food from the soldiers at the fort, but at least that was an army of men. You are an army of women. This is wrong, he says. This is bad medicine." Then, the young man's courage exhausted, he turned and trotted into the trees.

Rabbit reported it to Rain, who translated for Sister Irene. "What shall we do, Sister?"

Irene gave Rain one of those "what now" looks, then walked to a cauldron used in Army hospitals to boil bloody linen. "Let's make soup," she said. "It always works at the orphanage. The smell of soup can tame any man. Men love soup. Let's show them that we are an army of cooks."

In the weeks and months that followed, Creeks started to trickle in, small groups of women and children at first, with the men in the trees watching warily, like stag deer watching does enter a clearing. At first came the most vulnerable ones, with nothing left to lose. Irene noticed with a breaking heart how desperate, how frail and how hungry each successive group of displaced persons was. The women had trembling fingers laced with fear and famine. The children's hair had lost its sheen, their eyes were too big for their faces. Some of the very young had the distended bellies of starvation. "What kind of Devil's game is this?" Sister muttered to herself. "The hungrier they are, the more their bellies swell."

Soon the old men came, then whole families and broken remnants of villages; quiet, shuffling, each with a story of despair that some could express and some simply could not find words to describe.

Rain tried to break the gloom with humor. "Where are your moccasins, you forgetful girl?" she softly teased a youth of ten or twelve.

"I ate them," the girl replied solemnly. "We all did."

It was Christmastime in Montgomery, but the law offices of Farley and Abercrombie were far from festive.

Elihu Farley and James Abercrombie were the owners of the Alabama Emigration Company, a new entity with a single purpose: to move every single Creek man, woman and child out of that state overland to Memphis, where the Army would transport them by boat to Indian Territory. The company had been formed in response to two new, and annoying, developments.

First, Northern churches, led by the Quakers, while not openly opposing Indian removal, were insisting that it be accomplished as humanely as possible, and not at gunpoint. Second, newspapers, even some Southern newspapers, were turning against Jackson's ham-handed abuse of power. The Indian Removal Act had recently been struck down by the United States Supreme Court. Jackson imperiously answered that maybe the Supreme Court justices could interpret laws, but now he'd like to see them enforce them. He was going to get rid of the Indian, and the electorate was behind him. Still, Jackson didn't want to see front page stories of federal troops removing Indians with bayonets. So he signed an executive order to hire the Alabama Emigration Company to do his dirty work for him, and allocated up to a whopping $200,000 to do it. The company got twenty dollars a head to round up Indians, and twenty more dollars when it deposited them at Fort Gibson.

It should have been sweet, but many Creeks were headed the wrong way—downriver to Mobile where a few riverboats were willing to transport them to New Orleans and up the Mississippi for the same fee. Something was taking money out of the Farley and Abercrombie purse.

"Did you get the damn report? What in the hell is going on?" Farley barked.

"Don't go snarling at me, Eli. I'm not our problem," Abercrombie said. "Yes, my detective delivered his report to my home late last night, and you're not going to like it, not one little bit. He rode all the way up the Chattahoochee from Mobile to find out what's going on. It's a damn tent city rest station, hospital, hell, hotel that's attracting Indians like flies to honey. We burn them out upstate, and they hightail it downriver where they can stay for a couple of days, get fed, get blankets and stuff, and after they are all fat and sassy, they get carried by wagon down to Mobile, and we lose twenty bucks."

"Well, let's send a couple of the boys over there to rough 'em up a little. Tents burn, too, you know."

"Can't do it. They plunked down next to Fort Mitchell and the soldiers watch over them like lambs, day and night. Our boys are tough, but they're not stupid."

"We've got to do something, Jim. The governor tells me that the folks in Mobile are getting fed up. These Indians aren't just on the move; they're grazing like cattle. Try to buy a bushel of corn down there, it'll make your eyes water. Just who is this 'they' we are talking about anyway?"

Abercrombie actually chuckled. "I've been saving the worst till last. Believe it or not, it's a nun. The damn Yankee newspapers are calling her the Angel of the Chattahoochee. They are making her into a living saint. Sells papers, I guess."

Eli Farley was quiet for a moment. "Look, if we can't afford a bushel of corn anymore, how can she?

Where is she getting her medicine, her food, her blankets, her damn money? I've been watching money fly out the door for our trip to Memphis, and we haven't even left yet."

"I'll get the detective on it right away. In the meantime, you and I better hie ourselves over to the governor's office and let him know if he and President Jackson want this overland emigration to succeed, they by God better shut down Fort Mitchell. We can handle it from there."

Chapter Sixteen

John Coachman was exhausted, and demoralized. The forced evacuation of the Five Civilized Tribes west of the Mississippi was now a reality even he could no longer ignore. President Jackson's defiance of the United States Supreme Court had been the clincher.

Now, after more than two years denying the inevitable, he had very little time to set his affairs in order. His only real asset was Sunrise Farm and he needed to protect it for the sake of his clan and the dozens of orphan children still living in the mansion.

He contacted his old friend Thomas Grayson, and together they made plans to travel to Delaware to create a new corporation, Sunrise Capital Investments, with Marco, Brother Bart, Thomas and himself as the only stockholders. It would take a while for the farm to be incorporated, so John returned home with the difficult task of furloughing most of his stable staff. John held out hope that in less than two years Jackson would be defeated, the nation would come to its senses, and he and his employees could return to the stables just as before. Frankly, to maintain his sanity, he could hold no other belief.

Approaching Sunrise Farm at last, John looked with irritation at a carriage stopped in the center of the farm's whitewashed gate, blocking his entry. Standing on one side of the carriage was a rough-looking man in a black frock coat like an itinerant preacher. On the other side was a man in the garb of the Alabama militia, a rifle held at parade rest.

"May I pass, sir?" John said wearily.

"You are Mr. John Coachman, sometimes referred to by your Indian name Co-cha-ma?" the man in the frock coat asked in a voice most often heard in a courtroom.

"I am."

"Sir, I am Alabama Special Marshal Charles Dabney. Is there someplace we can talk?"

"Here is fine, Marshal Dabney," John said with just an edge. "I doubt that you will be here long."

"Nor will you, sir, I am sorry to say. I have official state papers here authorizing the confiscation of this farm and all surrounds currently in your possession."

John dismounted and tried to hold his temper. "Marshal Dabney, you are trespassing on my land. How dare you, sir? You have no standing here. This is Tennessee, not Alabama."

The frock-coated man's voice became oily. "That's where you are wrong again, Coachman, or whatever you call yourself when you are not pretending to be white. Among my papers is the official plat of the northern counties of Alabama. This farm is in Alabama and has been for more than twenty years. You can look at the map yourself if you wish. And all during that time, you have not paid a single penny in state taxes. You leave us no choice than to confiscate this farm." He slowly pulled back the right side of his coat to reveal a badge and revolver.

John kept his hands in plain sight. His voice became more friendly as the situation became more fraught. "As much as I disagree with what you say, perhaps we can reach an accommodation. How much do they say I owe?"

"I am afraid we are well beyond that stage. You owe nothing, because you own nothing. This farm is now the property of the state of Alabama."

"Then I guess I'll see you in court."

The militiaman barked a derisive laugh. Dabney also chuckled. "My goodness, this just isn't your day, is it? Didn't you know? An Indian has no standing in an Alabama court. He cannot sue, he cannot testify, he may not even legally enter a courtroom." Seeing John's arms partially raised and offering no threat, he pulled his coat closed again. His lips curled in a death-mask smile. "The state of Alabama does not wish to seem cruel, of course. You have three months from today to gather your belongings and accompany all those women and children I saw running around here to the new Creek emigration staging area near Huntsville. If you are unable or unwilling to obey this order, the Alabama militia is prepared to assist you. Good day, sir."

Major Edward Pratt sat at his desk in the headquarters of Fort Mitchell, drinking his morning coffee and rereading the official orders that had arrived in the weekly mail pouch from Fort Washington.

Major Pratt was a boyish-looking apple-cheeked Pennsylvanian from Lancaster whose rank commanded far more authority than his mien. He had grown a wispy moustache in a mostly unsuccessful attempt to add years to his demeanor. But what he lacked in gravitas, he made up for in intelligence and command logic. His men liked him, he was fair, and in this Godforsaken outpost with no Indians to repel and few Indians to protect, they were content to plant gardens and while away their time.

That was about to change.

Tapping the orders with a pencil, he called to his aide-de-camp in the next room. "Lieutenant Orrin, will you come in here, please?"

A young officer who looked even less field-tested

than the major entered. In fact this was his first assignment, and his boredom level was reaching new heights. Seeing the stack of papers on the commander's desk, his curiosity was piqued. "Yes, sir? Any news from headquarters? Any chance we are being reassigned to a tropical island?"

"Be careful what you wish for, Lieutenant. In fact we *are* being reassigned. Every damned one of us. They are closing Fort Mitchell."

"Can't say I'm surprised, sir. There haven't been any new troops assigned here for months. And why should there be? Sitting around here growing tomatoes and watching those poor hopeless Indians parading past us, and us with orders not to lift a finger to help them. It's against my better nature. It's just not right."

"Well, we won't have to watch them parade past us any longer, Orrin. The state of Alabama has been squawking so hard about the Indians eating them out of house and home, that not only is Fort Mitchell being closed, but the disembarkations from Mobile are being stopped and the Indians will no longer be allowed to emigrate south. Those poor souls, thousands of them, will now be forced to go overland across Mississippi and Louisiana up to Memphis. And our new assignment, you, me and the other sixty soldiers left here, is to accompany them, put them on riverboats and send them to, I don't know, Hades.

Why is it, dear God, why is it that soldiers trained for war have a better understanding of humanity than congressmen elected to serve it? Now walk with me, will you? I have to go tell a friend, the one they call the Angel of the Chattahoochee, that she is no longer welcome on the Chattahoochee. I am tasked with banishing an angel."

Chapter Seventeen

Major Pratt and Lieutenant Orrin respectfully walked their horses past the occasional cluster of rough, low to the ground huts they knew to be Creek cemeteries. Many of the Indians who made it to Sister Irene's tent town received warmth, food, and basic first aid before they were sent by wagon to the Gulf. But many came to the way station to die; not a few were dead when they got there. Sister Irene lamented that so many, especially the children, died of disease. A simple head cold which she and Marco would have shrugged off killed babies. Of course, it did not help that many were on the brink of starvation to begin with.

Entering the collection of tents, bonfires and huddled people, the two soldiers were impressed by how clean and orderly the makeshift village was. It was similar, yet eerily different from the typical Indian village. Except for some murmurs and groans, the place was quiet. No dogs, of course; they had been eaten long ago. No laughter and very little conversation; the people had retreated inside themselves. And yet the place did not seem hopeless like the gaggle of whiskey-soaked confused walking dead who surrounded Fort Mitchell when Major Pratt was assigned there last summer. There was at least the spark of humanity here, kindled by the Angel of the Chattahoochee and her assistants.

They passed the sick tent where Rabbit and Rain were replacing bandages, cleaning wounds, and adjusting blankets. There were plenty of blankets, thanks to the Army supply masters at Fort Washington, and even the suspicious chiefs now accepted them with gratitude. Major Pratt noticed that Rabbit and Rain touched the face or patted the shoulder of every person they met. They didn't learn this from Sister Irene; this was the Indian way, and some of the prim nuns at St. Matt's could have learned from them.

The officers dismounted in front of the larger tent, where Sister Irene was supervising a crew of women volunteers handing out gourd bowls of soup to trembling hands. Stirring a steaming cauldron with what once may have been a canoe paddle, Irene brightened when she saw Major Pratt. They liked each other immensely. He brought her newspapers from the North, and she provided him with conversation and living proof that the world was not insane after all.

"Welcome, Major Pratt, top of the morning to you.

Did you bring me anything to deposit into my *pulmenti mundi*?" She saw the younger lieutenant's quizzical look. "The learned Major here christened the soup *pulmenti mundi*, Lieutenant," she laughed, "because sooner or later almost everything in the world goes into it—beef, mutton, pork, rice, beans, barley, poke greens. You name it, I'll cook it." She turned back to the Major. "Well, Ed?"

"I'll have six cows driven to you this afternoon. They lost their milk, I'm afraid." He approached the nun and lowered his voice. "I am also afraid they are the last cows we have and no more will be coming. Enormous changes are on the horizon for both of us, Sister. Is there someplace we can talk in private?"

She saw the sadness in his eyes, and at a time that seemed that things could not possibly get worse, she knew suffering was bottomless. "Come with me to the wood shed, both of you," she said softly, taking Pratt by the elbow the way she used to lead the orphans to dinner.

"What is the matter, my friend?" she said at last. Noticing the younger officer looking over his shoulder, she added, "Don't worry about being overheard, Lieutenant. We are away from the people, and most of them can't understand English anyway. Tell me why you look troubled."

"Because I bring troubling news. Fort Mitchell is being closed and we, skeleton garrison though we might be, are being reassigned. We leave within the month."

"That is unsettling news for you, I am sure," Irene said. "And sad for me, as well. Beyond the comfort and safety the fort provided us, I have grown fond of your wit and your intelligence. Not to mention your carrots."

"There is more bad news, I am afraid," Major Pratt said. "My orders are to close you down as well."

She gasped, then sat heavily on a stump, clinching and opening her hands as she often did in times of stress. "But why us, Ed? We have done nothing."

"You have done worlds of good, dear woman, and that is the problem. The way station has become a magnet, attracting Creeks from all over. The state of Alabama doesn't want you here anymore. You are to be allowed to send one last wagon train of the blind, lame and infirm south. Then every able-bodied Indian here is to relocate to Huntsville for journey by land to Memphis and the territories. My new assignment is to accompany them on that awful journey, damn it all. Excuse me, Sister."

Their silence was broken by Marco galumphing into the shed with an armful of fresh-cut logs. He was dressed in the traditional Creek long shirt and leggings and his black hair was cut in the page boy style favored by Creek men at the time.

"Whoa, those are heavy," Marco laughed with a

puff of breath. "You need to lighten up on the bonfires, Sister. I had to walk a mile just to find a tree." Then he noticed the two Army men who had been obscured by the wood pile. "Good morning, gentlemen. I don't believe I have had the pleasure."

"Major Edward Pratt and Lieutenant David Orrin at your service. We are attached to Fort Mitchell." Pratt cut his eyes toward Sister Irene. "Temporarily. I've been to the way station many times, but don't remember seeing you. Are you working here?"

"Only temporarily as well, I'm happy to say. For the last three days, I've been bringing wood to Sister and she burns it. Not much future in that, is there? Marco Secundus, gentlemen, wrangler for John Coachman at Sunrise Farm when I'm not on vacation cutting wood."

"Oh, we know John Coachman, don't we, Major?" Orrin said. "A real gentleman. Do you suppose he'll be coming with us?"

Marco's eyes narrowed. "Coming with you?"

"Hell and damnation, Orrin," Pratt grumbled.

Irene stood and placed her hand gently on Marco's shoulder. Her voice was matter-of-fact. "Please allow me, Major. Marco, Major Pratt has received orders from Washington to close Fort Mitchell and escort all Creeks remaining in Alabama to Huntsville, for emigration cross-country to Memphis." Her voice caught just a little. "Part of those orders are to close the way station. It's over, my friend."

Marco whistled softly. "I am truly sorry, Sister. This seems to be the week to be cashiered. I just delivered the last herd of brood mares to St. Matt's. It's over for us, too, at least for now. Mr. Coachman has furloughed all of us—Uncle Hes-se, me, the stable boys. I'm a wrangler with no horses to wrangle."

"You must be mighty good if you're working for John Coachman," Major Pratt said. "It is a curious world, is it not. You are a wrangler with no horses, and I have a string of ponies with no wranglers. I wish I could hire you."

Still uncertain after his recent gaffe, Lieutenant Orrin almost whispered, "Government regulations won't let you hire an Indian, sir."

"Marco, I hope you don't hate me for this," Sister said, her hand still resting on his shoulder. "Major, I have known Marco since he was a foundling at St. Matthew's Orphanage in Cincinnati. He is no more Indian than you or I. Like many a young lad, he was fascinated by the tales of James Fennimore Cooper and, being an orphan, chose to live among the Indians, who accepted him with gusto. I am proud of your decision to do so, Marco, but you are not burdened by a stigma of birth. Major, did you know that Marco is so good with horses, the Creeks gave him the name Horse Talker? He is amazing."

Major Pratt brightened. "If both John Coachman

and Sister Irene vouch for you, I'd say my luck is changing. Would you like to hire on as my wrangler, Marco Secundus?"

Marco was thoughtful. "Well, if all the Creeks are being rounded up, I guess I'll be heading to Memphis one way or the other. I actually know that route. Mr. Coachman and I took it last year. It's a tough go, with swamps and rivers and mosquitoes as big as sparrows. But if I can be of help to you and my people, the answer is yes." He looked to Irene. "But what about you, Sister? What are you going to do? Go back to Cincinnati?

Now it was Sister Irene's turn to be thoughtful. Finally, she asked Major Pratt, "Are you familiar with the works of Francis Bacon, Edward?"

"I spent four years at VMI running away from him, I'm afraid."

"He was a brilliant man and a brilliant writer. One of his most famous essays was about the Turkish holy man Muhammad. Bacon quoted the prophet as saying 'If the mountain will not come to Muhammad, Muhammad will come to the mountain.' My path is clear. I will walk with you to Memphis."

Chapter Eighteen

The Alabama Emigration Company called it The Gathering Place, a benign name for a disaster.

The local men cluelessly rearranged the racetrack and fair grounds outside of Huntsville with food stations, fire pits and slit trenches, having planned on quartering 2,000 Indians; 3,000 tops. Sick, hungry, besieged and scared to death, 6,000 were herded into the makeshift camp, almost overnight.

It wasn't a gathering place, it was a vast hive of humanity—a hive with neither beekeepers nor queens. It was only a matter of time before the hive collapsed.

The creator of this hive, the state of Alabama, had never attempted anything remotely like this before, and its ineptitude was staggering. It grossly underestimated the amount of food necessary for 3,000, much less 6,000 captives. What meat that did show up was often tainted, stolen or bartered for whiskey. To keep theft to a minimum and to insure fresh beef, Emigration Company employees took to loosing cattle into the throng and letting nature take its course.

There were no crops, of course, and the Indians could not forage. They grew hungrier every day.

They also grew more confused. They became docile, often listless. Whiskey was partly to blame, but the hive had no leaders and no resolve. The Creeks had always looked to their chiefs for guidance and statesmanship, but those men were gone. The entire McIntosh group, with leaders like Rolle, Chilly and young Daniel McIntosh, had fled to Indian Territory years before and, ironically, after a year of decimation, had taken the best portion of the new land and was now thriving. Menawa was dead. The brilliant leader of the upper towns, Opathle Yahola, who first resisted removal, saw the wisdom of early volunteer emigration and led more than 2,000 Creeks to Mobile and passage to the new territory by riverboat.

In contrast, the chief of the lower towns, Eneah Micco, refused emigration and spearheaded a rebellious group of 800 hot-headed young men into the Florida everglades to join the Seminoles in defending land that nobody really wanted—insect-ridden and disease-infested swamps. Although there were skirmishes from time to time, white men didn't give a damn about the Everglades, and essentially ceded it to the violent and unpredictable Seminoles. But word of Eneah Micco's futile efforts was portrayed by unscrupulous whites as a "Creek War," which doomed the remaining peaceful and unsuspecting Alabama

Creeks to be herded like animals and banished.

Many other young men simply took to the woods. The Blue Herons and many of the Bear clan went north and joined Cherokee renegades in the hills of Carolina.

That left 6,000 men, women and children looking for a leader to comfort them.

Shakespeare wrote, "Some men are born to greatness, some achieve it, and some have greatness thrust upon them." In the summer of 1834, greatness went looking for John Coachman.

Coachman took his mother by carriage to Washington and Thomas Grayson. "Please keep her safe here, Thomas. When this ridiculous migration is over and we are settled in our new land, I will send for her."

Thomas took John's hand. "Of course I will, John. I will name her as an official interpreter for the Creek delegation here, which will give her immunity. And in time I won't just send her, I'll accompany her. It would be unseemly to represent a nation you've never set foot in. But what about you, my friend? You can, and should, be a member of our delegation. We need you here."

"Not as badly as I am needed at home, old friend. Thanks to you, my mother will be safe, but I have literally hundreds of cousins, near-cousins and clansmen who have depended on me for years. Sunrise Farm sustained us all, but now Sunrise is gone, and the weight falls upon me. I also feel deeply committed to my Aunt Rabbit, Sister Irene and that young nurse—Rain?—who worked so tirelessly to minister to our people on their way to Mobile."

"Sister Irene? She's the one they call the Angel of the Chattahoochee?"

"Yes, and she has already saved untold lives. She is devoted to the Creeks, especially our children. She is a marvel, Thomas, but occasionally her reach exceeds her grasp, as the poets say. My foreman, Uncle Hes-se, tells me she is hell-bent...." He chuckled. "Maybe I should rephrase that: determined to go across country with those poor hapless souls huddled in Huntsville. In a way, Mother and I got her into this fray. After so many years of denial, I feel I must make amends somehow. I will go with Sister and my aunt to Memphis and beyond."

John Coachman took one last look around the ghost village and stables that once were Sunrise Farm, gave Amber King a last frolic through the orchard which, ironically, was laden with fruit, and headed for the way station and the only friends and family he knew.

The way station was itself in transition, coming down like a circus leaving town. He saw Sister Irene and the officer he recognized as the commander of Fort Mitchell directing soldiers to fill two wagons with tents, supplies and blankets. Uncle Hes-se, who had agreed to drive one of the wagons, and Marco were tending to a surprisingly large string of horses and mules.

Seeing John Coachman approach, Sister Irene came skipping toward him. "*Hensci*, Co-cha-ma, *hensci*," she sang.

"Speaks English, Latin and now Creek?" Major Pratt exclaimed.

Irene laughed. "It's the only word I know in that impossible language. Well, impossible for me, at least. Marco seems to thrive on it."

"Have to," Marco said as he took John Coachman's hand in greeting. "I'm still studying to be an Indian. Uncle Hes-se tells me that I speak like a Creek child … which he says is a big improvement." He nodded to the big man now holding Amber King's reins. Uncle Hes-se nodded back, more in acknowledgement than understanding.

"Is your mother safe?" Sister Irene asked.

"Absolutely," said Coachman. "She's now part of the Creek delegation in Washington." He laughed. "It's nice to know that at least one member of my family is working. Need a mule skinner, Sister?"

Now it was Irene's turn to laugh, albeit ruefully. "Uncle Hes-se has filled that unpaid position, my dear friend. But you are cordially invited to ride alongside. We intend to take a little walk to the Indian Territories. The Army has sent us packing." She turned to Major Pratt. "Not that you had any choice, Edward, I understand that."

At that, the officer saluted Coachman, then extended his ungloved hand in greeting. "Major Edward Pratt at your service, sir. Your reputation precedes you, Mister Coachman. It is a pleasure. Please accept my condolences to you for the loss of your horse farm. Marco tells me it is, or was, the diadem in the crown of horse breeding in this country. The shoddy treatment you have received at the hands of those Alabama politicians is unforgivable. If it were within my power...."

Marco simply could not remain quiet. "Mr. Coachman, they will be sending us overland to Memphis on almost exactly the same trail you and I took with poor Chief Menawa last year. Major, you are looking at the best horseman in Creek country and one of the few men who knows how to lead us to Memphis. Couldn't you hire him on as scout or something? He will save us time, and no doubt save lives."

Major Pratt hesitated. "Well, it would be an honor, of course, and what you say has merit. Perhaps by using your English name, we could...."

Uncle Hes-se, who had clearly understood far more English than previously thought, flew into a speech in his native tongue that would make any Indian orator proud and leave no doubt as to its importance. "Horse Talker is a fine young man, but today you should not listen to him. He says the soldiers can use you. That is true. But Co-cha-ma, your people can use you also. We can use you like a baby can use air or a fish can use water. We can use you because without you we will die. We have spoken about this. The People know you. The People trust you. You have been across the big river. You have seen our new land with our eyes. You hold our future, the future of our children, in your hands. Your people need a leader, Co-cha-ma. Without you we are nothing. You must be our chief. I have spoken."

John Coachman looked with a hint of sadness toward Sister Irene, then turned back to Uncle Hes-se. "I hear you, my friend. Our people need a leader, so I must follow. Go to Huntsville and tell them if it is their will, I will stand."

Chapter Nineteen

John Coachman, Co-cha-ma, agreed to serve as leader of the lost swarm of humanity only until they reached Indian Territory; then he would relinquish his role to Opathle Yahola, who would be settled in the Creeks' new home months before this group made it to the Mississippi River. He refused the title of chief, but accepted micco, which translates somewhat ambiguously to "head man."

There was no ambiguity about his position as leader, however. The hundreds, perhaps thousands, of Creeks who stood respectfully chanting his name that humid August day outside of Huntsville expected leadership, and desperately needed it. They were worn out, not in body, but soul.

Co-cha-ma found an able friend and ally in Major Edward Pratt. The Indians of that day, especially the full-bloods, lived in the present. Their days, moons and years were more or less the same, with planting and harvest, abundance and scarcity arriving in turn. There was no need to plan for the unknown. The past, the future and the present were bundled together. But this arduous journey of a thousand miles and many months was an unknown, and military men like Major Pratt knew to plan for it or die.

Co-cha-ma, Marco and Edward Pratt met with the representative of the Alabama Emigration Company to set the trail to Memphis. Departure could not be a moment too soon for the Major, who feared an outbreak of cholera in the insect-ridden and increasingly filthy camp.

"In a way, Alabama did us a small favor by placing us here in Huntsville," Co-cha-ma said. "We are north of much of the misery. We can follow the Tennessee River west for three hundred miles. That not only provides us with plenty of water, it gives us a high road that will avoid most of the Mississippi swamps. This will still be a terrible journey, but at least this way we have a chance."

"You've got more than a chance with my men, Chief," said Big Bill Coleman, leader of the drivers. Coleman bordered on the obese and didn't look like he could sit a horse for long, much less endure 800 miles on a buckboard. "Those ol' boys know how to make them mules dance, and that's a fact."

"I hope it's a plain old two-step," Major Pratt said flatly. "I heard you've had a deuce of a time finding drivers, even offering parole to prisoners who claim experience. Your men need training, and that, too, is a fact. Are they here yet?"

"You shouldn't ought to talk that way," Coleman pouted. "Yes, we got them staked out over near the prison, and no jokes if you don't mind. Two hundred men and a hundred wagons ain't no laughing matter. But we'll get you to Memphis in no time."

"No time?" Major Pratt snorted. "I just hope we don't die of old age before we get there. I've moved troops in wagon trains before. Under the best of conditions, with soldiers in good health and used to following orders, it is hard to average more than ten miles a day. And these aren't the best of conditions. And these aren't soldiers. We'll be lucky to do half that."

"All right, let's plan for five miles a day," Co-cha-ma said. "That will get us into Memphis before the new year. If we are lucky, we will be on the river before the worst weather hits, but it will still be a long, cold slog. Major, we will need Sister Irene and her nurses more than ever, I fear. Can you help me place them on the trail?"

Pratt chuckled. "Thinking ahead. Good for you. That's thinking like a soldier, sir. Yes, Marco and I have discussed this. We have three full wagons. We will put one wagon, tents and supplies fifty miles out, and another fifty miles beyond. Then when the last people pass the first station, we will situate it another fifty miles further, and so on."

Big Bill Coleman lit a cigar. "You said you had three wagons. What about the third one?"

Marco said, "That's the supply wagon, with medicine, bandages and blankets."

"Blankets in August. Tits on a bull."

"Those blankets will turn into shoes and clothing soon enough, Mister Coleman," Marco answered politely. "And it won't be August forever."

Buck Tom, the Creek lawman, approached Marco shyly. "Horse Talker, I do not want to bother you, but I need your help. I think you know that five of my lighthorsemen and I will go with the people to the new land. We will be there to keep the peace, and," he paused to find the words, "when mister whiskey comes to camp, to protect us from each other. But our powers are not clear, even to us. We can catch a whiskey seller if he is Creek, destroy his whiskey and give him to the micco for punishment. But if he is white, all we can do is run him off. We can deal with theft among our people, but again, if we try to arrest a white thief, he will shoot us and no white court will touch him. I don't think the soldiers know about us, and I don't want them to shoot us, too. Will you help me meet the head soldier?"

"Of course I will, Buck Tom," Marco said. "It pleases me that you and your officers will be with us.

You were very helpful on our expedition last year, maybe even saved my life. Come with me. The head soldier's name is Major Pratt. He is a good man. I trust him."

Major Pratt sat at a field table near the entrance to the garrison tent, filling out one of the myriad government papers that made many Army officers rethink their careers. He saw Marco and a tall man in his namesake buckskin shirt approach, both with arms high in greeting. Pratt stood and made his way around the front of the table.

Marco put his hand on Buck Tom's shoulder. "Major Edward Pratt, I would like you to meet Buck Tom, captain of the lighthorsemen, the Creek police. They will be accompanying us on our journey."

"Your reputation precedes you, sir. You are a welcome addition to our exodus." Major Pratt saluted and then offered his hand in welcome. Buck Tom, like all Indians, was unfamiliar with this white man's gesture, but offered a weak hand in return as a show of respect.

Marco continued, "Major, Captain Buck Tom speaks little English and he has asked me to speak for him. He says hunger and whiskey are bad bedfellows, and we will need the lighthorsemen to settle disputes and keep the peace. To do so, the lighthorsemen will be carrying weapons—rifles and side arms. Captain Buck Tom wishes that the soldiers not confuse his men for desperadoes. He therefore respectfully requests that you not shoot them."

Major Pratt roared in laughter. "Tell him that he drives a hard bargain. No, don't translate that. I am glad he has come. I understand. We can fix things just fine. We will issue the lighthorsemen with the same arm bands we issue our scouts, blue and white arm bands that can be seen for miles." He laughed again. "Please assure the captain that if I shoot him, it will be on purpose, not by accident. No, don't translate that, either. All this paperwork is making me as silly as a school girl."

Walking away, Marco said, "See, Captain, he is a gentleman. Your men will be safe with the major as your friend."

Buck Tom grunted. "Yes, I am relieved. And although I speak little white man language, I understand some. Please tell the major that he is a funny man, and if I shoot him, it will be an accident."

Chapter Twenty

In early September the Alabama Expedition Company wagon train got off to a bad start and went downhill from there.

First, the wagons, purchased sight unseen by the federal government through unscrupulous agents, were mostly used, worn and in need of repair. Only forty of the wagons were covered. There was one blacksmith, and he was no Brother Bartholomew.

Second, the expedition company expected 2,000 Indians, more or less, with 20 per wagon. It got 6,000, and even with thirty crammed into each wagon, half were on foot, slowing things down considerably. Co-cha-ma ordered all adult males to walk unless they were feeble, blind or very ill. Compliance was no problem; Creek women might not have been able to stand as chiefs, but in many ways the clans were matriarchal, and the women were highly vocal in deciding who should and who shouldn't ride. Captain Buck Tom pulled a few men off the early wagons, who then got such a sustained tongue-lashing they ran to the back of the train to hide their shame.

And last, there was a trail along the Tennessee River, but it was of necessity narrow and tree-lined, requiring the wagon train to proceed single file. The train almost immediately fell victim to the "accordion effect," where those at the end lagged further and further behind. And with oxen, mules, some horses and cattle (at least at first), there was no scurrying to catch up. By the fifth day, the train was two miles long. People at the end often found that the food that had been laid out in the morning was gone.

Whiskey joined the wagon train almost immediately.

It simply cannot be overstated how vulnerable Indians were to whiskey. Marco saw its horrifying effects first hand among the Creeks huddled around Fort Gibson, but filed it away in the wake of Menawa's attempted assassination. Only a few days out of Huntsville, however, while rounding up some ponies that had broken their hobbles, he almost rode his horse over three Creek men with an empty whiskey bottle. They were so drunk they were lying in the wet grass, unable to stand. The familiar stench of whiskey and vomit jarred Marco's memory, and he hurried back to Co-cha-ma and Major Pratt to report the violation.

"How in the hell did they get it, Marco?" Major Pratt asked. "I know they didn't bring it with them. I inspected every wagon myself as we broke camp. And they don't have any money. Is it the drivers?"

"I don't think so," Co-cha-ma said quietly. "Big Bill is a braggart and exaggerator, but he's no idiot. He's not going to pay his men until the end of the trail, so if they get caught selling whiskey, he'll kick them off without a penny."

The Major nodded. "Just the same, I'm going to put some of my men in their camp every night. They are a rough bunch. And I wouldn't put it past them for pilfering. Your provisions are meager enough, Chief, without somebody trading them for whiskey."

"Somebody," as Buck Tom soon found out, turned out to be Indians. Just before dawn one rainy morning, he stumbled across four men carrying sacks of rice and beans. When the men saw him, they dropped their booty immediately and sat on the ground with heads bowed like naughty children. They said they were headed for a trading post they'd seen the day before to trade the stolen goods for what they called *wehoma*, red water. "We have done it before," one of the men admitted, holding his hands up for absolution. "The food tastes bad, and the white man gives us much red water."

What they didn't know was that they were bringing back something even more deadly than whiskey; they were bringing back white man diseases.

*   *   *

It would be hyperbole to call the Creeks' trek to the Mississippi River a death march, but there was death, death everywhere. There was so much death that it became commonplace, banal.

At first the clans tried to prepare their dead properly, wrapping them in canvas or blankets, building little huts and then sitting with the dead as they passed to other realms. But it quickly became apparent that sitting for the traditional four days was impossible, and then they saw that whatever blankets and sheeting were still available would have to be shared among the living. Bodies were placed in mangrove swamps, wedged under branches to keep them from being eaten by animals, and abandoned.

Hearts grew heavy. Death was part of nature, of course, but this was something new. Many of the elders, men more often than women, simply lost the will to live. Everything they had known—every tree, every rock, every stream—was gone. Creeks were farmers, not hunters, and many of them, especially the women, never travelled more than ten miles from where they were born. Sometimes at sunset, when the wagons stopped and people went looking for firewood for the evening fire, a few would wander off, lie down by a river or stand of trees, and wait for death.

As the nights grew longer and colder, the people

would huddle around campfires for warmth and reassurance. This proved to be a mistake.

Sister Irene, Rain and Rabbit would take turns in the evening visiting the campfires to teach the women how to prepare the unfamiliar and meager provisions like salt pork, fatback and barley. Major Pratt, using an old Army trick, provided the women with bags of cayenne pepper to show how to mask the taste of tainted meat.

The three women would return exhausted to Sister Irene's medical tent, where she and Co-cha-ma would play chess while Marco and Major Pratt would take turns reading aloud from newspapers that arrived in the mail pouch from the nearest fort.

One chilly night in October, just after the harvest moon, Rain entered the tent sniffling, her blanket pulled to her face. "Sister, I would like to stay in the wagon tomorrow, if that is all right. I am very tired and also very hot. And my nose, what do you say, waters."

"Why, of course you can, dear girl," Irene said. "Here, let me have a look." She pulled Rain's blanket back to reveal red blotches on her neck. Irene scowled. "How long have you had this?" she asked.

"A few days, it is nothing." Rain replied. "It itches because I am so hot. Do not look at me so, please, Sister. I have a cold, nothing more. I probably caught it from those children in the far camp. They have colds, too. Give me a day to rest. Then I will tend to the children."

"No, my dear, you will not. We've seen this before, haven't we, Marco? At St. Matt's two years ago? The children didn't give you a cold. You have the measles."

"It's been going around my men, too," said Major Pratt. "Half my men have been on call this week. Stay in bed for a couple of days and drink plenty of water, you'll be feeling better in no time."

Chapter Twenty-One

The Creeks don't have a word for angel because their spiritual world doesn't contain any such beings. So they called Sister Irene the White Woman of the Chattahoochee.

Nineteenth century Indians had a habit of placing caring and trustworthy whites in high regard, perhaps because they encountered so few of them. After those years at the way station and more than a month on the trail, Sister Irene was almost venerated. Ironically, although the Creeks didn't believe in a god that healed people, they suspected that Irene could.

These Indians didn't expect much from their medicine men in any case. A shaman's mystical pouch, his powders and potions, his incantations and songs, were comforting to people who agreed that it was better than nothing. When someone recovered, as some must, the medicine man was quick to remind people that his powers had worked with Old Man Little Mouse, so if they didn't work this time, it just might be the patient's fault.

Sister Irene refused to take credit for people who recovered, which—Rabbit reminded everyone in earshot—made her powers even stronger. The people understood. They brought her barren women who wanted to have babies again. They brought her crippled old men hoping she would help them walk. And they brought her children with measles.

Down through history measles has been the most pernicious of infectious diseases. The virus is airborne, and hearty. It seems to seek out children. It is very slow to present; people can be carrying active germs for as long as ten days before they begin to show symptoms, symptoms which in the early stages seem like nothing more serious than a cold or sore throat. Then come the blotches and rash, the difficulty in breathing and swallowing, the spiking fevers and often, especially among the Indians, death.

There was very little Sister Irene could do. The only medicine she had, provided to her by Major Pratt, was calomel, a mercury-based chunk of blue crystals that would be mixed with water. The mixture was inexact, which didn't matter, because fifty years later Army doctors found that at best calomel was ineffective, and at worst could introduce mercury poisoning into the blood.

But Irene and her helpers did what they could. She gave the patients copious amounts of water, dosed them with calomel, applied cool compresses, and prayed.

Many people died, but some people got better. And Sister's reputation grew. But there was one person on the trail who had completely lost faith in Sister Irene and her God. That person was Sister Irene herself.

Measles probably entered the Creek exodus of 1834 through white whiskey sellers who infected the drivers, who in turn took it back to their wagons loaded with the infirm, women, and children. It killed more than 400 people by the time the snows came.

But it didn't kill Rain.

Rain was young, Rain was robust, and from the moment she walked sniffling into that tent, she inherited a nurse determined to will her back to health: Marco.

Marco was absolutely convinced that he loved Rain, but expressing these feelings befuddled him. He was an island of ignorance in a sea of hormones. The orphanage hadn't groomed him for it. The nuns had been no help, of course. And the only women he met as a child were those who rejected him. Brother Bart occasionally broached the subject of women, but befitting his past life as a pugilist, Bart could be a bit earthy, and he often spoke in rough terms about women walking past the stables. Marco set his sights higher.

Marco had seen engravings of men and women

kissing, and thought he would like to try that. But he didn't know if you were supposed to ask permission first, or what words you should use. He also wasn't sure if Indians kissed; he certainly hadn't seen any evidence of it. But he had seen Rabbit and Rain comfort the sick by patting and stroking them, and the idea of getting close to Rain, touching her, filled him with desire—which he gallantly changed into lofty words of sublimation. He would be Natty Bumppo to Rain's Alice Munro, Ivanhoe to her Rowena.

Marco knew firsthand the fever dreams that measles caused, and he imagined that sweet moment when Rain's fever would break. She would look deeply into his eyes as he tenderly daubed her dry lips with a moist cloth and whisper "My hero."

He asked Major Pratt to be relieved of duty for a few days to care for Rain. The request was readily granted.

"You didn't have to do that, Ed," Sister Irene said the next day. "I can easily care for Rain just as I care for the others, and I've already had the measles."

"I know you could, Sister, but I granted Marco leave for three reasons," the Major answered. "First, there isn't much for a wrangler to do on the trail. This exodus can be many things, and boring is high on the list. I want to keep him occupied. Second, Marco probably knows by now that he works for the Army but isn't in it. His request was just a courtesy; he could have done it regardless of what I said. Which brings me to the third and most important reason. I've been watching Marco sidle up to Rain every chance he gets, and I watch her respond. Marco can give that girl something beyond you and me: reason to live."

Marco made a bed for Rain in the equipment wagon, and she soon fell into a deep sleep. He wrapped her in two of the remaining blankets, under the "chicken soup" home remedy of the time that sweating was good to drive out impurities in the blood. It is also true that measles often brings chills, so the poor victim can be burning up one minute and freezing the next.

He kept watch around the clock, giving her sips of water, cool compresses for her forehead and cracked lips. Although he was more or less a stranger to the hominy-based soup called sofki, he knew it was a staple of the Creek diet, and asked Rabbit to bring him bowls of it. After two days of feverishly refusing the soup, including one episode where she threw up on him (an act he had not included in his knightly fantasies), she weakly took a few spoonfuls.

At daybreak on the fourth day Marco must have nodded off, because he reawakened to see Rain quietly looking at him and smiling.

"I knew it would be you," she said gently. "I saw you in my sleep."

"Hello, Rain," Marco said, more formally than he

had intended. "Is there anything I can do for you?"

"Yes. Will you help me stand? I need to make the water." Seeing his perplexed look, she made the request again in Creek, using a word Marco had never heard but instantly understood.

Marco stood holding a blanket high as Rain squatted beside the wagon. This was far from his "my hero" dream, but everything seemed so natural to Rain that his embarrassment ebbed.

Rain crawled back into the wagon, her eyes never leaving Marco. "You saved my life," she said in Creek. "I am happy." She smiled. "I would like to be your woman. Do you want me, Horse Talker?"

This was so much better than his Natty Bumppo scenario, Marco felt almost dizzy. A woman, a beautiful woman, had accepted him. He tried to imagine how John Coachman might answer, but he was adrift. He was glad they were speaking in Creek. He might have fainted in English. "Yes, yes I do. You are my woman. We will go to the new land and make a new life." Then he laughed and added in English, "But let's not tell our children what brought us together."

Chapter Twenty-Two

"Do you pray, John?" Irene asked, studying the chessboard.

The first snow of the season was falling that evening, just a dusting and not very cold. It probably wouldn't stick, but it threw a blanket of hush over the temporary way station, sending everybody to sleep except the famous insomniacs, Sister Irene and John Coachman.

"Depends on what you mean, I guess," John said, moving his bishop out of harm's way. "If you mean pray like a Catholic, the answer is no."

Irene pulled back from the board just a little. "How do you know how we Catholics pray?" The question sounded too confrontational to Irene's taste, so she chuckled and quickly added, "Have you been spying on me?"

John laughed as well. "My spies are everywhere, it's true, but no. I learned about the Catholic faith from a man who had fallen from it: my father. He claimed to be a Jefferson deist, whatever that is, and he rebuked all religion as hokum. He held Christian prayer in special low esteem, I'm afraid."

He took a pull on his pipe. "I am glad we are having this conversation at last. I admire you so much, and yet I too have no use for your religion. I have felt like a liar around you, lying with my silence. I want to fully answer your question, but to do so requires a bit of family history.

"My father's harsh assessment of religion had exactly the opposite effect on me than he may have intended. I was young, and like most young men, I rebelled against my father. I was also looking for something, I don't know what, something to make sense of the world swirling around me.

"I began going to other churches, growing less convinced that what I was hearing was true. Finally one summer, I guess I was seventeen, I snuck away to a revival being held in a tent out in the woods near town. The preacher shouted and threatened, told us we were all sinners, we were born sinners, and we would burn in Hell and damnation unless we gave our lives to Jesus, and our money to the preacher. I became repulsed and angry in equal measure."

"I have seen such men," Irene said quietly. "They are false prophets. You should ignore them."

"Well, I did more than that. I could not believe that there would be a God so mean as to condemn us sight unseen. Instead of hating my father, I thought he hadn't gone far enough. So I turned to my mother for answers. She showed me the spiritual path of the Creeks, and I found comfort in Creek ways, a comfort that has grown as I get older."

"I'm afraid I will have to take issue with your assessment of God as mean," Irene said, but John noticed that she cast her eyes away from the chessboard and into the far corner of the tent. Then she turned back to him, meeting his gaze. "And you haven't exactly answered my question. But I am curious: what is the Creek God like?"

"This may be confusing," Co-cha-ma said. "We don't have a God per se, nor even a word that conveys such a powerful person. We have something that you would call in English the Creator, Ibofanga, but it is a presence, neither man nor woman, and it has, um, what should I say, an associate, or assistant, the Master of Breath.

"Many white scholars think the Master of Breath is our God, but he is more like the weather: unpredictable, sometimes forgiving, sometimes cruel. They are not gods, nor do they sit on a throne in heaven. We have no Heaven. Heaven requires a Hell, and we don't believe in Hell. We don't believe in sin. We believe in good and bad."

"You don't believe the bad should be punished?"

John moved a knight. "That brings us finally to the subject of prayer, doesn't it? I'm sure you've heard someone say 'God damn you?'"

"Of course. That is blasphemy."

"But isn't it also a kind of prayer? Isn't that asking God to punish the enemy, send them into damnation? We Creeks don't blaspheme; it would be useless. The Creator creates and moves on, the rest is up to us. We do not ask Ibofanga to vanquish our foes or visit misfortune upon the rascal who stole our horse." John paused. "But just as we don't believe Ibofanga or the Master of Breath would intentionally hurt, nor do we believe they can heal. We don't pray to be cured. Can't you see how fraught with sadness such a belief would bring? If God can heal a child, why does He allow some to die?"

Irene stared at the man, her pretty face bathed in the warm glow of the lamp. Her eyes grew wide and quickly filled with tears. "Oh John, somehow you knew, didn't you? I stand among the sick, the helpless and the innocent; more than I ever hoped to see in two lifetimes. I pray day and night for their recovery and the babies keep dying. They all just keep dying. That's why I asked you the question. I don't know how to pray any more. I am a nun, I am married to Jesus; I wear his wedding ring. And yet somehow I feel we have turned our backs on one another. I am losing my faith, John. What am I to do?"

John took her hands in his. "Forgive me, dear woman, but one cannot keep faith with a God that is inconsistent. We can only have faith in each other. And I have abundant faith in you. I have seen you steadfast and fearless, gathering your babies around you like a she-bear. I have seen you dole out loving touches and sofki in equal measure. And finally, I have seen you fill the heart of a man who thought he had no heart. I will say no more."

Irene looked down at her hands in his and blushed.

Chapter Twenty-Three

A seedling will split a rock to reach its destiny as a tree. A flower will push through a New York sidewalk to reveal its brief beauty. And love will crawl out of the mud to walk to Indian Territory.

That winter in Mississippi was as gray as gun metal and relentlessly wet. The glue-like mud was so deep it made a sucking sound when you lifted your foot. Wagon wheels often sank axle-deep, making even five-mile days impossible.

Yet after five months on the trail, life had gained a sort of squalid equilibrium. It was cold, but not cold enough to freeze to death. There was hunger every-where, but the starvation that had come earlier to visit the old, the frail and the very young had done its job: it had killed them. The measles took what it wanted, then moved on.

Down through time, Indians had always accepted good times and bad, and these were bad times. Everybody was hungry, everybody was cold, everybody was tired. But every now and then you could hear the old medicine drums break the silence, every now and then there was bubbly laughter coming from a wagon at night, and in the mornings children began to play.

And there was love among the ruins. Marco and Rain presented themselves to Co-cha-ma, Uncle Hes-se and other elders to declare that they were husband and wife. Co-cha-ma told Marco that he would now be Raven clan, just as his wife, and told the gathered Creeks to accept this man and woman as family. Major Pratt, resourceful as ever, presented the couple with two Army blankets and a pup tent, which was all the dowry Marco and Rain would ever need.

Irene sheepishly approached Marco and asked if he wanted her to bless the marriage. "Yes, Sister," Marco said. "Rain and I are truly married, but I lived at St. Matt's too long to close that chapter of my book. And it's as Brother Bart used to say: belt and suspenders."

"That's fine, Marco. I will include the two of you in tonight's prayers." She paused. "And from now on, I'd prefer to be just Irene. The Creeks don't care one way or the other, and I would find more comfort in it."

At least in dress, Irene had no problem downplaying her role as a nun. The two sets of nurse uniforms she had set out with were long gone. She now wore a doeskin dress given to her by Haya-Atke when they were still attending to babies at the manor house. She hadn't worn it then, thinking it a bit too fancy (Haya-Atke had made the mistake of saying this was the type of dress often given new brides), and had been afraid that it might be seen as abandoning the church. She gladly wore it now for warmth and to blend in. With her jet black hair in braids and her sun-weathered face taking on the same mahogany color of those around her, she looked Indian right down to her shoes, which were a sturdy pair John Coachman brought her back from Washington.

John Coachman's gentle words had not been lost on her. He had opened his heart just a crack and it thrilled and frightened her. She was naïve in many ways; she had been a nun for eighteen years, but she remembered her father snorting that another man had one year of experience, repeated ten times. When it came to the heart, was that her? She didn't know what to think, so she decided to quit thinking and take St. Francis' advice and "listen to God."

Through John's insight, she came to understand that asking God to curse a man or cure him were simply opposite ends of the same continuum. And that continuum was forged from selfishness and pride. Our God will bless us if we pray long enough, our God will be pleased if we sing His praises loud enough, we … we … we control God by our piety. And worse, she knew that many Christians believed that the Indians had brought their suffering upon themselves because they were heathens. She hadn't lost her belief in God, she finally realized; she believed that He was a wrathful and idiosyncratic child. She decided to forgive herself, to let the admiration of a fine man like John Coachman wash over her, to bask in the laughing seeds of hope and love that lodged deep within every child. To laugh herself. She rose and walked outside her tent to greet the morning. Later that day, she would teach the children how to play ring-around-the-rosy.

Marco had never been happier in his life. It was Rain, of course, but it went so much deeper. He had lived his early life upside down. He was born into a society that professed family values, only to be cast aside. As noted earlier, there were no orphans in the clan; aunts and uncles were just as likely to teach you, to feed you, or to scold you as your parents. Aunts were even called *manage*, little mothers. And the power of the clan was enormous. The first question Creeks asked upon meeting was *"Nagin gee-maleghee dadee?"* What clan are you?

He was also impressed by the logic and equanimity of Creek life. He had left a world run by men where women couldn't hold office, become a doctor or lawyer, or vote, to a shared world. Indian men ran the tribes because tribes go to war, but women ran the clans because clans are family. Men and women both voted on their tribal leaders.

And Marco learned to his delight that Creeks didn't hold virginity to the same controlling, and often punishing, degree of white men. It wasn't that Creeks were promiscuous; it was just that sex was natural, and fun.

A few months after their marriage, Marco and Rain sat by a stream, splashing their feet like children. "Because of you, I am truly a man," Marco said. "When we get to Indian Territory I want us to have many children, strong children."

"You may not have to wait long, my love." She touched her belly. "The seed has been planted, I think. I believe the harvest moon will bring us babies as well as corn."

Marco jumped to his feet. "Perfect! A new family for a new world. You will teach our child the Sacred Path, the ways of the clan, and I, well, I will teach it to talk with horses and whites."

"Same thing," she giggled.

Chapter Twenty-Four

For every Marco Secundus who left the orphanage whole and hopeful, there was probably at least one Mickey Noonan.

Mickey regularly seethed with a fury he could neither identify nor shake. The one thing he knew for sure was that nothing was his fault. He hated St. Matt's. He hated the nuns for punishing him just because he wanted to show the younger boys who was boss. They banished him to the stable for being "too rough."

The stable was worse. He hated Brother Bart and his disapproving eye. That old bastard never came right out and said it, but Mickey could tell Bart thought he was dumb. And Jesus Christ, it was always Marco did this and Marco did that and Marco did the other. He hated Marco the most.

He was annoyed at the men in coats and starched collars driving their carriages past the stables with their high-toned ladies. And those whorish ladies, he imagined they were laughing at him behind their fans.

Someday he'd show one of them bitches his fine Irish manhood and she'd drop to her knees in praise.

His only relief was drinking cheap wine down on the wharves. Even that was kind of annoying, because he couldn't bring any back to the stables for a little nightcap like a regular fellow.

So late one drunken night, he impetuously grabbed Brother Bart's carpetbag of shoeing tools and some pennies and dimes Bart kept in a drawer for making change, and ran away for good, thinking he'd by God start his own stable. Mickey was never very good at making plans, however, and this one had two flaws. First, he wasn't very good at shoeing and second, he hated horses.

Mickey wasn't very bright but he could be cunning on occasion. Sober, the very idea of being a black-smith repulsed him. Besides, he'd burned his bridges this time. But he thought he could use the carpetbag full of tools as an entry fee to join one of the gangs that worked the river. He had shared a bottle or two with Sleepy Thornton, even done a little thugging for him, so he hid out until nightfall, then made his way to the Captain Ristey, a saloon Thornton was known to frequent.

Sleepy Thornton was a twitchy, almost frenetic, tall man with the face of a ferret and a droopy eyelid. He and his gang, the Nightcrawlers, worked up and down the Ohio, stealing merchandise off the docks at night (the midnight mercantile, Sleepy called it), rolling drunks, breaking and entering, fighting and drinking.

Mickey walked up to Sleepy and dropped the fifty-pound carpetbag at the man's feet.

"Well, if it ain't Mick the Mick," Sleepy said. "What the hell you got in there? You selling anvils?"

"A present for you, Sleepy. Must be a hunnert dollars' worth of smithing tools in there. I'm thinking of getting out of the blacksmith business and joining up with you and your boys. Try to pick up that bag. You'll see I'm worth my salt."

Sleepy made a half-hearted one-handed stab at lifting. "Woof. Well, I never had any doubts about you being strong, Mick. And I could always use a little extra muscle. The other gangs working the river, some of them ain't as nice as I am. But like any fine gentleman's club, the Nightcrawlers got some rules." He counted on his fingers. "First, I'm the brains of this outfit and what I say goes. Second, no killin'. The cops are willing to live and let live as long as I keep them greased, but a body floating in the water don't do nobody any good. Third, we split things even, except I get ten percent on top for reading and writing and being the boss. If you can abide by those rules, then I'll welcome you to the family. You in or out?"

"In," Mickey said, his chest swelling with pride. He had never been asked to join a family before.

*   *   *

Sleepy Thornton spent late mornings drinking laced coffee and reading newspapers. The newspapers mainly served as testimony to his intellect and power in the gang, but he did read them. And very often what he read pissed him off.

"Goddam Indians. First they won't leave, rampaging all over the South, threatening our womenfolk, then Andy Jackson says 'pretty please' and they say okay, but only if you give us about a million acres across the Mississippi and boxes of gold." He stabbed the paper with his finger. "Says so right here. I just don't get Jackson sometimes. He calls himself an Indian fighter, then he says all the Indians got to be—what is it?—removed, and then he kisses them on the butt and gives them boxes of gold as a going away present. And I'm talking boxes of gold, thousands and thousands of dollars. I don't get it." He looked across at Mickey, who had become something of a bodyguard and lap dog in the months since he joined the Nightcrawlers. "You know any Indians?"

Mickey hawked up a laugh. "I know a make-believe one."

Without taking his eyes off his paper, Sleepy grumbled, "Yeah, I used to be a make-believe pirate. Are you even listening to me, dumbbell?"

"Yes, boss," Mickey said, red-faced. "But this one

is a real make-believe Injun. His name is Marco and he used to be in the orphanage with me. Then he goes studying up on Injuns, then declares he's going to be one and hightails it down south, leaving me holding the bag. And he was so damn dumb he didn't but hardly get down there than the Indians give him some title, make him a big muckity-muck, so like he's a real Indian now. And then the government says fine, cut your own throat, and sends them all packing at bayonet point. Last I heard he was walking across Alabama with a squaw in one hand."

"And maybe a bag of gold in the other. Maybe he's about as dumb as a fox. Maybe he read the same things I've been reading about Old Hickory paying the chiefs off in gold coin. Maybe he decided to work his way inside and help himself to some of that shiny stuff. Why else would a white man go live among the Indians?" He dropped the paper and started pacing. "I got a funny feeling that if we could find your old buddy Marco, we'd also find the gold. We might as well relieve them of it. There ain't nothin' to buy where they're going anyway. Do you know where he is, Mick?"

Mickey narrowed his eyes in an attempt to look shrewd. "Not exactly. But I know somebody who does, my old boss at the stables."

Chapter Twenty-Five

Brother Bart sat in the soft glow of a kerosene lamp, tallying the books for his monthly report to Mother Cornelia. It was a chore he didn't relish, and he often let his mind wander. He remembered fondly the days when Marco did this task for him, and in half the time.

He looked toward the half-opened stable door to see a hulking figure silhouetted against the night sky. "What on earth? Mickey, is that you? Come back to turn yourself in to the police? Bring my tools with you?"

Mickey stepped just inside the door, opening his hammy hands in supplication. "Now, Brother Bartholomew, there is no need for finger pointing. I know nothing of any tools. But I admit I left here in haste and anger. And I further admit, and here I seek your forgiveness, sir, that in my anger I took two dimes and seven cent pieces from your money drawer. It was the wrong thing to do, and I have returned to make reparations." He pulled a silver half dollar from his breast pocket and tossed it on the table in front of

Bart. Bart made no move toward the coin, but kept his hands free and his eyes focused on the man-child.

"As much as we all rejoice in the repentant sinner," Bart said affably, "this seems a rather curious time to regain the path of righteousness. There is always plenty of daylight for the honest man. What's the real reason you are here?" He paused and stared into the darkness. "Who's that with you, Mickey? Show yourself, sir."

Mickey puffed with pride. "That is my employer and, how do you say, my college, John Edward Thornton."

"Shut up, Mick," came a low voice from the shadows.

"'Sleepy' Thornton? Oh, yes, I've heard of you, sir. Your reputation as a scoundrel is well established. Poor Mickey. As the Bard says, lie with dogs, arise with fleas. Why have you come? There is nothing of value here."

"We seek only a little information, sir," Sleepy said in his basement voice.

"What kind of information?"

Mickey drew near the table, so near Bart decided to stand. "Like I said, I've learned a lot from Mr. Thornton, and I want to make my reparations. I also owe some money and my hand in gratitude to my old friend Marco. The last time I saw him, I treated him poorly, I think. I want to find him and renew our brotherly friendship before he goes to the Injun lands. My heart is heavy, Brother Bart. Please tell me where he is. I must see my old friend again."

"Your heart is heavy? About as heavy as the purses of gold some of the newspapers say the Indians are taking across the Mississippi? I don't know where Marco is, and even if I did, you would be the last person I would tell. Why don't you and Mr. Thornton go back scurrying along the wharves where you belong?"

"You misjudge me, as always," Mickey said coldly. "I'd dearly love to stand here all night and listen to your lies, but Marco is awaiting. You know where he is; that Injun-loving nun of yours writes you letters from somewhere. She knows where he is, and so do you. Give me them letters before I lose my temper. I'm warning you, this ain't the same Mickey Noonan you used to boss around." He took another menacing step forward.

The slur on Sister Irene lit a fuse in Bart. "She is not my nun. Curb your tongue, boy, or you may find yourself talking through broken teeth. Get out, the both of you."

"Call me boy, will you?" yelled the infuriated Mickey. "I'll take them damn letters, you little monkey, and give you this in return." He took a powerful but wild swing at Bart, who easily side-stepped him and gave him a cautionary cuff on the ear.

"Mickey, don't make me do this. I used to be a prizefighter, remember?"

"You're just an old monkey-man now," Mickey grunted, and swung again and again, each swing blocked by Bart.

Bart was no fool, however. Mickey had fifty pounds on him and more than once Bart had seen a slugger's luck overcome skill. He decided to cool Mickey's ardor. The next time Mickey came flailing in, Bart caught him square on the nose, breaking it and sending blood flying. Mickey screamed in pain. "I'll kill you, I'll kill you!"

Bart fended off a few more blows, but even some of Mickey's misses were catching Bart painfully on the arms and shoulders. It was time to end it. He backed up half a step, circled to his left, and knocked Mickey senseless with four or five well-aimed jabs and hooks. Mickey fell like a bale of hay.

"Well done, sir," said Sleepy Thornton, waving a small silver pistol at Bart. "If you ever decide to change professions, come see me. In the meantime, I'll thank you for those letters."

"Whatever letters I may have are personal, Mr. Thornton," Bart said evenly. "And anyway, by the time I get a letter, weeks have passed and the Indians are long gone. My letters will do you no good; they are at best history, sir, a stained history of starvation, disease, sickness, death and profound sadness. How anyone could possibly believe there is gold hidden among those poor people is beyond my—"

In the dark behind Bart, Mickey came to, wobbled to his feet, grasped the two-pound hammer Bart used for shoeing from the tack table, and swung it like a cudgel. It hit the smaller man's head with such force that Bart flipped forward over his table, landing with one eye grotesquely protruding from its socket. He was dead before he hit the ground.

"I got him, I got him," crowed Mickey.

"No killing, you big baboon!" a furious Sleepy Thornton shouted. "We don't have time to get rid of him now, it's almost daybreak and we're a mile from the river." He waved his pistol in front of Mickey. "Truth be told, I've cooled a bit on the subject of Indian gold. Our late friend may have spoken the truth, and now in any case I would no more go on a job with you than I would dance with a grizzly. You are bad medicine, you dumb ox. Get yourself killed if you wish, but get out of my sight. And get out of Cincinnati; the cops will figure it's you." He turned and disappeared.

Mickey started crying as he ran. Thanks to Bart and Marco, he thought, he'd been kicked out of the only family he'd ever had.

Chapter Twenty-Six

John Coachman had a white man's problem. It was a large problem, a familiar one, one he could see coming a mile away, but he couldn't do a damn thing about it.

To the incurious observer, things had never looked better for the Creeks on the trail. Spring had come at last to the South with its astonishing array of flowering trees and bushes. Winter's diseases—cholera, flu, even measles—had gone back into hiding, and the lead wagons were less than fifty miles from Memphis with its promise of riverboats and rations.

No, the problem lay elsewhere. John had been on horse drives where men had gone half loco on payday. And payday was looming, with an added twist. After six months on the trail hauling people they considered beneath them, even subhuman, the wagon drivers, known as skinners, would fulfill their contract when they reached the Mississippi. Two hundred men with a single ambition: get paid, get drunk, get laid and get the hell out of there. How they took their leave, and perhaps their contempt, worried John deeply.

He decided to take his concerns to Major Edward Pratt. It comforted him to see that the constantly moving field tent that was Major Pratt's command post was up and in military readiness as always. This was more than a tent to the major; this was his citadel of authority. Pratt was a well-educated and tactful man who had always shown respect for Coachman's position as head of the People. But he left no doubt that if there was ever a difference of opinion, his would prevail. He played chess; he read Shakespeare. But he had orders to see the Creeks safely to Memphis. He would brook no man who stood in the way of this mission.

"Good morning, John," Pratt said loudly, waving his arm in an arc over his head. "These Southerners know how to cook up a right fine spring morning, don't they? How may I be of service? Had your coffee?"

"You have coffee? I've been hanging around the wrong tent. All Irene has is coal soap to swab sore throats. Yes, I'd like some, if it's no bother." John accepted one of the ubiquitous blue and white-speckled metal mugs that were standard Army issue.

"Ed, I've heard it said that the last mile of a journey is the most dangerous. People take their minds off the tasks at hand, I guess. Looks like we're finally reaching that last mile, and I am worried. Dark clouds are forming, I'm afraid."

"You think some of your people will do something stupid, John?" Major Pratt asked, shaking his head. "I don't. There's no liquor on the train and no money to buy any. We're making good time, we're getting better rations now that we are getting near to Memphis. Why, Marco and I even saw what he called a ribbon dance last night at camp. We're into the home stretch, as you horsemen say."

"It's not my people I'm worried about, Ed. It's those Alabama skinners. Many of them openly don't like us. I've heard them use vulgar words and seen them make threatening gestures. Thanks to you and your men, they have stayed in check. They know if you report them, they will get kicked off the train without a penny. But that's about to end. When they hit the docks of the Mississippi, they are going to get paid, and paid well. I'm afraid they will turn into men who have been at sea too long. And every single one of them has a sidearm. Those were the rules when we left. I had to abide by them."

"What'll we do with the drunken sailor, early in the morning," Pratt singsonged unenthusiastically. "Yes, my men have reported warning signs from the drivers for days now. Much is just campfire bravado from the young roosters, but much is darker, as you say. That's why I have my soldiers bivouac with the skinners every night. Those drivers may have sidearms, John, but they are no match for my trained soldiers, and they know it." He leaned over his coffee mug and lowered his voice. "Look, I know your lighthorsemen are armed, but they are few. Just to be on the safe side, select some men you trust, one to each wagon more or less and have them report—just a few at a time, mind you—to Sergeant Turnbull, my supply master. He will issue them each a repeating rifle and ammunition. Tell your police to keep the rifles out of sight. It's against the law to provide a firearm to an Indian; in my case a court martial offense."

"Thank you, Ed," John said, sliding his empty cup across the field table. "I will tell Uncle Hes-se to keep them well hidden, and let's hope we never use them." He felt no need to tell the Major that the new rifles would be stored under false bottoms in the two medical wagons, along with the dozens of rifles and pistols already present.

Mickey only briefly felt remorse about killing Brother Bartholomew. He had to talk himself into blaming the little man for being mule-headed. Hadn't his refusal to tell them about Marco been just as good as admitting that big shit and the other chiefs were holding gold, and plenty of it? So it was Brother Bart's pet that got him killed. Well, good. He'd find Marco and kill him, and bring Sleepy Thornton a box of gold coins, where he would be welcomed back like that prodigal son the nuns kept yammering about.

It was daylight now, and Mickey could hear the clangs and whistles of the Irish Catholic police combing the streets to find the bastard who killed one of their own. He kept running.

Mickey knew that his best avenue of escape was the river. But despite having lived his entire life less than a mile from the Ohio, he couldn't swim. He started running west through the tenements and warehouses that encroached on the river. He had to think. Maybe he could sign on to one of the barges headed downriver. Maybe he could steal a fishing boat. He could catch fish, he thought, although he never actually had. Maybe he could even get work on one of those elegant stern-wheelers making its way down to Louisville and Cairo and, who knows, New Orleans. Maybe killing Marco would have to wait. Maybe he'd become a riverboat gambler, make lots of money and come back to Cincinnati and tell Sleepy that there was a new boss in town. And Sleepy would say yes, Mick, you're the daddy now.

He hid and ran all day and the next night, and formulated a small plan. He'd find a fish camp and dock where the riverboats stopped to take on water and wood, go downriver and circle back like he was coming from the west, not Cincinnati, and say he was looking to go back home. His mama was sick, he'd say, so he'd be willing to work for vittles, just this one time.

Sure enough, a day later he spotted a riverboat on the horizon. It looked kind of beat-up to Mickey. If he hadn't been upwind, he could have smelled it before he saw it. It was a dung-sides, so called because it hauled cattle and hogs all the way down to Texas to breed and strengthen the local longhorns and razorbacks. The crew had long gotten used to the stench and, Mickey soon discovered, brought a strong fragrance of their own to the mix.

But it was a ticket out of town, and the captain was willing to take the muscular young man on. Somewhere in the back of Mickey's mind, he saw that the move from the stables to the dung-sides was half a step down, and he blamed Marco for this, too.

It took seven days to travel the Ohio to the mouth of the Mississippi at Cairo. Mickey caught on quickly; he was, after all, doing pretty much on the river what he had done in the stables. The smell didn't bother him, he liked the other men okay, and the food was simple but plentiful. The riverboat would tie up every evening, and while the men put on water and wood, and even pretended to clean out the pens, their boss, a man named Big Charlie, would go into a general store inevitably situated near the wharf and buy bread, sausages and buckets of beer. Big Charlie could read and write, so he also bought a newspaper from whatever town they were passing—Pittsburgh, Cincinnati, Louisville, Memphis. Then he'd read the news to the boys as they lounged and smoked after dinner. Mickey liked this very much; it reminded him of pleasant evenings at St. Matt's where the nuns did the same before bedtime. Looking back on it, maybe Mickey didn't hate the nuns so much. They were strict, but evenhanded. You knew where you were with them.

Big Charlie read better than the nuns. He'd stand, he'd stamp his feet, he'd wave his arm in the air. At least once a night, it seemed, he'd get tickled and shout "On the barrel head" and "God's truth." Big Charlie didn't get angry much; mostly he'd just punctuate some of his readings with a shake of the head, a laugh and a hearty "horse manure." He wasn't trying to rile anybody; he knew exactly what he was doing:boring his men to death until they fell asleep.

However, one night just a few miles out of Cairo, Big Charlie read an editorial from the *Memphis Appeal* that stirred Mickey into acute awareness. "Well, listen here, boys, if this don't beat all: 'The Indians are coming, the Indians are coming,' it says here. This is funny. 'Lock your doors, lock your pantries, hide the dog under the bed, here come the Indians. Don't worry, they don't want your scalp, they want supper. More than a thousand of them, hungrier

than grasshoppers, munching their way across
Alabama, Mississippi and Tennessee, eating squirrels,
tree bark, every blade of grass, not to mention half the
salt pork, bacon and corn in the state, courtesy of
Andy Jackson. Give them a wide berth, give them a
wave goodbye, but don't give them a bowl of stew.
You'll have them hanging around your house like a
hound dog.

"'Seeing these bedraggled ragamuffins in person
lays waste to the rumors that crop up from time to
time that they are carrying gold out of the country.
This writer probably has more gold in his teeth than
those wretches have in the whole tribe. So let them
pass. Let them be on their way. Let them leave this
nation whose laws they never accepted. Let them go
to their own land that we, the citizens of the United
State, give them free and clear. Let them go, and let's
hope that the next Indian we see is on the cover of a
dime novel.'

"Pretty good writing, if you ask me."

"Pretty darn good," Mickey said, trying to keep his
voice calm. "Sounds like something worth seeing. Big
Charlie, I'm thinking I'd like to stay on all the way to
Memphis, if that would be all right."

Big Charlie didn't mention the story of Mickey's
sick mother, which he had probably known was a fib
when he first heard it. "Sure, Mick. You thinking
about going down there and cutting yourself a squaw

out of the herd? Well, why not? You're a young man. Won't hurt nothing."

Mickey's eyes grew steely. "It's a hell of a lot more than that. Those rumors about the gold? They are God's truth, Big Charlie, God's truth. I got it from a dying man, a man of the cloth, a man who knew. That's why I was on the river. There's gold coins, boxes of it, in that tribe all right, and I know exactly which man can lead me to it. But I'm going to need a little help. Feel like getting rich?"

Chapter Twenty-Seven

Big Charlie had been a skeptical and reluctant accomplice to the hot-headed Irishman from the start, and what he saw as they floated down to Memphis set his jaw.

The dung-sides had to dock a mile downriver, as always, to keep the flies and stench away from the townsfolk. As they walked the river road back to Memphis, Big Charlie counted eleven empty river-boats bristling with soldiers. "I hope Mick is good on his feet," he mumbled to himself. "He sure ain't getting out by river." Without even noticing it, Big Charlie had already changed "we" to "he."

When they got to the docks, every wharfside saloon and whorehouse was chock-a-block with some of the roughest characters he had ever seen. These weren't river rats, as Big Charlie and his crew called themselves. These were muleskinners, hundreds of them to Big Charlie's eye, mean on their best day, drunk with a pistol in one hand, raising hell.

Last, and most curious to Big Charlie, there wasn't

an Indian in sight. How do you steal gold from people who aren't there?

"Tell you what, Mick, old man. Your invisible Indians may just be brimming with invisible bags of gold, but to my way of thinking, your chances of being scalped are only slightly better than your chances of getting beaten up and murdered by those rowdy fellows yonder. And if you make it through that thicket, them soldiers are just itching to throw you in the stockade." He pulled a few coins out of his pocket. "Here's a little something for your troubles. I know you said you'd work for free, but I'm a God-fearing man, and setting you loose with nothing but your red hair would be a sin. You are a hard worker, and you are welcome to come along with me and the boys to Texas. All we got to contend with there is Mexicans and she-bears. But if your mind is made up, then we'll say good luck and goodbye."

Mickey slid the money into his pocket without a word of thanks. "I got business here. Personal business," he grunted. He turned and started walking upriver.

The stockade at Fort Memphis would not have had any room for Mickey in any case. It was filled with Creeks.

The fort, soon to be renamed Fort Pickering, was

huge, controlling every boat, scow and raft on the Mississippi. In some ways Fort Pickering was the fulcrum for the war that was teetering on the horizon, even then. The fort's garrison, already at odds with the state militia, was made up of Union soldiers from the North, who proved as sympathetic to the Indians as the Southern militia men had been condescending and mean. It has been said that no one values peace more than the soldier. Perhaps, too, soldiers respect the fragile beauty of life more than most civilians because they tread so close to the horrors of death.

Major Pratt had sent word ahead that the caravan was in bad shape, hungry, ill-clothed and sick; but the pitiful trail of humanity had to be seen to be fully absorbed. The fort commander, General Theo Stephens, was aghast. Stephens was a devote Christian whose wife had once served as a missionary among the Cherokees in the Carolinas. Through angry tears, Stephens ordered that every blanket, every boot, every sack of flour, anything that could be worn or eaten, immediately be taken from the store- houses and distributed to the People. Major Pratt, Co-cha-ma, the lighthorsemen and Marco worked alongside the soldiers distributing the bounty. Flour became flatbread, blankets became dresses, and boots became the source of good-natured joshing among wide-footed men who had only worn moccasins all their lives. Jubilation was not a feeling common to the Creeks, but it took no practice. Whoops, yips and giggles turned the stockade into a county fair, with foot races, braziers sending aromas of childhood into every corner, and grown women splashing each other with pans of water just because they could at last. Soldiers walked among the Indians handing out horehound pieces, lemon drops and peppermints.

The fort stockade turned into a Creek way station, where the People cleaned the tragedies off their bodies and souls, while the soldiers and local blacksmiths repaired the wagons, greasing wheels, tightening rims, replacing sideboards, and mending tack. The decision was made to put the undernourished horses and mules to pasture in Tennessee, restore them to health, then sell them to buy replacements when the riverboats reached Indian Territory. Marco stayed extremely busy with tinctures, liniment, oils and soothing words to the straggling stock that had been suffering and dying right along with the People.

Sometimes words and ointments weren't enough. Marco hated ending a horse's life, but sadly, he had become necessarily good at it. Perhaps he was the only somber Creek at the fort, and he lived for the moment he could return to Rain and her knowing, soft touches.

One morning Marco took his mug of coffee to Irene's medical wagons. They were tied up near the fort infirmary, where they were being refitted and restocked for the long river journey. There he found

Irene, Rabbit and Rain wrapping bandages and chatting in English and Creek, with Rain acting as the Rosetta Stone. Their comfortable laughter transcended language. Marco wanted to join in the laughter, too. "Hey, Sister, if you happen to see an Army doctor around here with a saw, run for the hills. There's a Dr. Sawbones inside who almost cut old Chief Menawa's leg off." The women squealed in mock fear.

"Well, I'll be damned," came a murmur from the underbrush. "I've got you now, Mister High and Mighty, I've got you now."

Chapter Twenty-Eight

Before Marco's arrival, Mickey had been lying in the bushes for hours; not so much in wait as confusion. He kept looking at the fort, hoping an idea would emerge. It hadn't.

Finding the Creeks had been relatively easy. He saw empty wagons being driven to the riverboats below, and backtracked until he got to the stockade. As usual, his plan was rudimentary, violent and vague. He would find Marco somehow, make him tell where the gold was, then kill Marco and take the gold back to Sleepy Thornton to be hailed a hero.

He'd been there since before dawn, watching Indians pass in and out of the stockade gates. This surprised Mickey, who thought the Indians were supposed to be prisoners. His confusion grew as he saw three women emerge from a large tent next to the stockade and stand in front of a long table, wrapping bandages and giggling like school girls. The young one was kind of fat (Rain was pregnant, but Mickey had never seen a pregnant woman), and the pretty one with the long black braids looked strangely familiar. But that was impossible; he had never seen an Indian before, either.

Mickey had a pistol that he bought off a drunken skinner, and thought of shooting Marco right there. But that would get him no closer to the gold, and like so many of Mickey's man-child plans, contained a flaw. Like a dragon standing watch over a pot of gold, Mickey was comforted by the gun, but had no idea how to use it. It would come to him, he figured.

Then as he watched, Uncle Hes-se joined the group, loaded the women onto a nearby medical wagon, and headed to the docks for boarding onto a waiting riverboat. After they departed, Marco turned back to the stockade, leaving Mickey deep in foggy thought. He couldn't follow Marco into the stockade. Him against a thousand Injuns? No thank you.

Then an actual plan bubbled up. That pretty woman with the braids was Sister Irene, he'd lay money on it. Didn't Brother Bart say she and Marco were hobknobbing with the Injuns somewhere down south? Why, Mickey wouldn't have to go find Marco; he'd let Marco find him, and die. He'd hide in that big tent and take the women hostage for bait, then when Marco came to the rescue, Mickey would make him tell where the gold was. Then he would kill Marco, and maybe take Sister Irene for his woman, to boot. He'd never done it with a nun before (he'd never done it with anybody before, but that didn't slow his fantasies).

Mickey stayed hunkered down and watched for another hour to make sure the medical tent was empty, then snuck into the tent and made himself comfortable behind a pile of blankets near the back wall. And he waited.

But Mickey was no good at waiting. He grew fidgety and irritated, jumping and pulling his gun at sounds real and imagined. He was hungry, he was bored, and he had to pee. He figured he could take care of the last item, at least, and peed into the blankets in front of him. He had never realized how pungent urine could be, and he started waving his hands and blowing at the stain so the smell wouldn't give him away.

He was still hard at work drying the blankets when the tent flap flew open. Mickey peered between the piles of blankets, but instead of the giggling women he expected, he saw a tall man. The man hung a lantern from the main tent pole. It cast everything in soft yellow, and the man sat down on a small upended barrel before placing wooden chess pieces on a board laying atop a field table. Then the braided woman who was probably Sister Irene came in and patted the man affectionately on the shoulder. "Ready for your next lesson in humility, John?" she said with a lilt.

Coachman adjusted the pistol in his belt and bent

over the chessboard. "I'm feeling lucky tonight, my dear. Here. I'll even let you start." He held out a white pawn, which Irene accepted, her fingers lingering a bit on his palm.

I'm gonna tell on her, Mickey thought. Nuns ain't supposed to make eyes at men. He was jealous and thought he should kill this man, too.

Then the object of Mickey's hatred came into the tent. "The ponies are hobbled and fed, Mr. Coachman. Everything's quiet. I've got next, okay?" He paused. "What's that funny smell?" Marco said.

Mickey saw the revolver in its Army holster hanging on Marco's hip, and decided that the element of surprise was about all he had left going for him. He came out from behind the blankets, leveling his pistol at first this one, then that one. "It's the smell of death, Marco; your death unless you do exactly like I say."

Marco gaped. "Mickey? Mickey Noonan?"

"You know this stinking sack of manure?" Coachman said as he carefully got to his feet.

"Shut up," Mickey shouted. "You're next."

Marco moved slightly to his left for a clear shot if necessary. "Yes, I know him. This is Mickey Noonan. He and I were at St. Matt's together. What's going on, Mickey? How did you find me?"

Nervously swinging his pistol from Marco to Coachman, Mickey tried to force a laugh that died in his throat. "What's going on is Injun gold. You tell me where it is, I'll let you live. And as to finding you, that was easy. The late lamented Brother Bart led me right to you."

Irene rose slowly from the chessboard at the word *late.* "You killed Brother Bartholomew?" she said flatly, her voice three notes lower than usual. She took a step forward. "Did you learn nothing at St. Matt's? Thou shalt not kill. Give me the gun, Mickey."

"No!" Mickey wailed and jutted the gun in her direction. It went off, and the bullet hit Irene in her upper chest, spinning her to the ground. John Coachman flung himself onto Irene to shield her from further harm. She lay there, not moving.

Mickey looked stupidly at the pistol in his hand. "I didn't mean to. I didn't mean to. It just went off."

By this time Marco had cleared his gun from its holster and he aimed it at Mickey. He hesitated. "I can't," he whispered, almost in prayer.

"I can," Coachman said. He turned, pulled his pistol from his belt, and shot Mickey Noonan, killing him instantly.

The fort hospital was literally only a hundred yards from the medical tent. They got Irene to the doctor within seconds.

"You are going to be all right," the doctor told the now-conscious Irene. "You're in a lot of pain, I know, and I'm afraid you are going to be in some more. I've got to get that bullet out of there. I'll give you a little laudanum for the pain; it should help. Who knows, maybe you'll even take a little nap."

"Thank you, Doctor," Irene said jauntily. "But if I do fall asleep, promise me you won't cut my leg off."

"Your leg?" said the baffled doctor.

"Yes, no sawbones for me. I want to stand on my own two feet when I marry this man," Irene said and squeezed John Coachman's hand.

Despite their concern, Coachman and Marco looked at each other happily.

Epilogue

On June 14, 1835, John Coachman and Irene Rippy were married by the chaplain at Fort Memphis. Major Edward Pratt was assigned to accompany the still-convalescing bride to Washington, D.C., where she would be reunited with old friend and now mother-in-law Haya-Atke. The two of them would make a home in the nation's capital. John Coachman had been chosen by Chief Opathle Yahola to replace a much-relieved Thomas Grayson as representative of the Creek Nation in negotiations with the federal government. Coachman also arranged with Uncle Hes-se to bestow a belated wedding gift of Amber King to Marco and Rain.

But first John Coachman, also known as Co-cha-ma, would fulfill his promise to accompany those Creeks who made the Long Walk to Indian Territory. The journey from Memphis by riverboat and wagon was almost a month long, but mostly uneventful. And when he, Marco, Rain and Rabbit arrived at Council Hill—soon to be renamed Okmulgee—they were in for a surprise.

Awaiting them was a hospital, a school, a mill, meeting houses and, to Marco's delight, a stable and smith. Dazzled, Marco looked to Co-cha-ma for answers. "How is this possible? We have just arrived. Is this magic?"

"Wrapped up in hard work and a bit of luck," Co-cha-ma answered. "Yes, we are new here, but Opathle Yahola and a thousand of our people made the trip down the Chattahoochee to Mobile and up the Mississippi two years ago. Even some of the McIntoshes have reached out in friendship. We are the People again."

"But these structures are new. Where did the money come from to build them? Certainly not from us."

"Your cowardly and murderous old friend was partially correct, but he got his geography all wrong. There was some gold—not much and not nearly enough to repay our loses—but enough to get restarted. We knew the white Southerners would try to steal it, so it was hidden in the false bottoms of Opathle Yahola's two wagons. Some critics thought that wise old chief was abandoning our people when he left early, but he fooled them."

With a little financial help from Co-cha-ma, Marco secured a lease for the blacksmith shop. Rain served as a nurse at the hospital when she wasn't having children of her own. They had four all together—

Irene, Bart, Dawn and Johnny (also known as Osten, which is the number four in Creek).

Of the 6,000 Creeks who took the Long Walk from Huntsville to Memphis, 4,200 made it to their new home in Indian Territory. By 1845 the Creek Nation was 11,000 strong. And the corn grew again. And the children giggled.

The End

About the Author

Jack Shakely is a fourth-generation Oklahoman of Muscogee/Creek descent.

After a successful career as head of one of the largest philanthropic foundations in California, he returned to his first love of journalism. His novel *Che Guevara's Marijuana and Baseball Savings and Loan* won the prestigious Oklahoma Book Award in 2014. His novel *The Confederate War Bonnet* was awarded the gold medal in two categories, historical fiction and midwest regional fiction, by the National Independent Publishers' Association in 2009.

Shakely lives in Rancho Mirage, California.